Your Highly Sensitive Child

Dr Aoife Durcan is a Chartered Counselling Psychologist with over a decade of experience working with adults, children and families. Her expertise lies in supporting those navigating complex mental health challenges and trauma, and the unique needs of highly sensitive individuals. She holds a doctorate in Counselling Psychology from Trinity College Dublin. Aoife is a sought-after speaker at international conferences and is deeply committed to empowering individuals and families to thrive.

'Aoife's personal experiences of being a 'sensitive child' offer a unique perspective of what it's like to 'be' like that and how they might see the world. As well as informing the reader in an insightful and accessible way, Aoife tackles some pertinent issues to help us to understand how to better understand sensitive children. This book allows parents to support their sensitive child without trying to harden them or coerce them into some form of robust resilience. Instead she offers us an understanding of their emotional world, which allows us to have the insights to offer useful and effective support to sensitive children.'
Colman Noctor

'This book is a gift and a gamechanger for parents of highly sensitive souls.'
Caroline Foran

'A must-read if you are a sensitive person or are parenting one. Full of insights, tips and techniques, this important book is a roadmap for anyone who is or is parenting a sensitive person. I highly recommend this book.'
Joanna Fortune

Your Highly Sensitive Child

Helping your child flourish in an overwhelming world

DR AOIFE DURCAN

GILL BOOKS

Gill Books
Hume Avenue
Park West
Dublin 12
www.gillbooks.ie

Gill Books is an imprint of M.H. Gill and Co.

© Aoife Durcan 2025

9781804581582

Designed by Bartek Janczak
Edited by Emma Dunne
Proofread by Tamsin Shelton
Printed and Bound in the UK
by Clays Ltd, Elcograf S.p.A.
Typeset in Minion Pro and Albra Display by
Palimpsest Book Production Ltd, Falkirk, Stirlingshire

*The paper used in this book comes from the
wood pulp of sustainably managed forests.*

All rights reserved.
No part of this publication may be copied, reproduced
or transmitted in any form or by any means,
without written permission of the publishers.

To the best of our knowledge, this book complies in full with
the requirements of the General Product Safety Regulation (GPSR).
For further information and help with any safety queries,
please contact us at productsafety@gill.ie.

Information given in this book is not intended to be taken as a replacement
for medical advice. Any person with a condition requiring medical attention
should consult a qualified medical practitioner or therapist.

A CIP catalogue record for this book
is available from the British Library.

5 4 3 2 1

*For Oscar, Ollie and all the other sensitive little souls.
To all the parents out there just doing their best,
I am right there with you, and I am holding
you all in my heart.*

Contents

Welcome to a walk through the mind of a sensitive child   1

CHAPTER 1: Understanding your sensitive child   5
CHAPTER 2: Your child's window of tolerance   27
CHAPTER 3: Our own life history   55
CHAPTER 4: How we learn to protect ourselves   79
CHAPTER 5: Temperament, being 'shy' and understanding anxiety   107
CHAPTER 6: The empath   141
CHAPTER 7: Criticism and 'being good'   165
CHAPTER 8: Navigating painful emotions   191
CHAPTER 9: Understanding our strong-willed children   213
CHAPTER 10: Sensory sensitivities   239
CHAPTER 11: My wish for every parent   257

Further resources   271
Bibliography   275
Acknowledgements   281

Welcome to a walk through the mind of a sensitive child

Highly sensitive, spirited, empathic, deeply feeling … These are all descriptions of children who feel the world on a deeper level. These wonderful children might also often be described as determined and strong-willed. I am sure you know exactly what I mean if you are reading this book, as you are most likely the parent or caregiver of one of these special souls. Described beautifully by Dr Thomas Boyce as 'orchid children', these delicate children (or seemingly not so delicate sometimes, for those of us with more spirited orchids) come into the world with a nervous system that is more intense, more reactive and finely tuned. They have big hearts and a nervous system that processes deeply, so as a result they feel every feeling from the tops of their heads to the tips of their toes.

As incredible as these children are, the reality is that parenting them can feel a little challenging sometimes. This is because it often requires a huge amount of 'digging deep' by us to understand and help them with their emotions. And they have *a lot* of emotions. They often like to be in control and can become frustrated and overwhelmed more easily in the context of change. They also just need a little more time – feeling rushed or being subject to too many competing demands can feel stressful for them. New situations often take time for them to adjust to, as these little observers take in so much from their environment, meaning they may experience overwhelm more often than their peers. They can be impacted greatly by criticism, tricky peer dynamics and ruptures in relationship with us. This can be really difficult to manage if we are under-resourced and exhausted ourselves. I work with the kindest parents who are often simply burnt out from life stress and pressure that is too much for *any* nervous system. It helps us considerably as parents to understand what is happening in our children's internal world and how their more intense emotional expression often makes sense.

Let me start by telling you a little about myself and the work that I do. Having completed my primary degree in psychology and subsequent master's in applied psychology, my learning journey continued in the Trinity College doctorate programme in counselling psychology. I have been fortunate to have studied with and been supervised by some of the most eminent thought leaders in the field of mental health.

I work as a senior psychologist in a mental health hospital in Dublin with adults experiencing complex mental health difficulties. One of the greatest privileges of my work is to walk the pathway of recovery with those who have endured painful life experiences and trauma, and those who are coping with acute or chronic mental health diagnoses. I see the harsh reality of the impact systemic factors – being isolated, unsupported, abused and neglected, and financial and housing instability – can have on human beings. The big-hearted souls I meet have gone through so much suffering, and often those deep-feeling hearts of theirs are left painfully wounded and sore. But I also see their resilience and capacity for healing with empathy, connection and support.

My research on child development and my everyday clinical work have shown me that the early chapters of our life story can have an enormous impact on our sense of self and the way we view the world. This is particularly important for the more sensitive among us, as the research clearly shows these children are more impacted by their environment than their less-sensitive peers. This has informed the focus of my private practice, where I specialise in working with sensitive children and their families and sensitive adults who are struggling. I am passionate about empowering this cohort to tune into the gifts and strengths of a sensitive heart. I also have so much empathy for parents. Navigating the world of sensitivity can be challenging without understanding and encouragement. I resonate hugely with the understandable overwhelm that comes with parenting and managing daily life. So many parents I have worked with felt afraid to ask for help for fear of being judged. My goal when working with families is to create a supportive and non-judgemental space while, most of all, helping them feel listened to and understood. I believe wholeheartedly that we all are just doing the best we can with the resources we have.

On a personal level, I too am a highly sensitive person. I experience the world around me so deeply that I not only empathise with others on a cognitive level, but I also physically feel their feelings. This sounds like a strange concept, but I have grown to appreciate the gifts and complexities of this way of being in the world. I am also a mom to two wonderful little boys, both of whom rank highly on the sensitivity scale. They inspire me daily, and it is fascinating watching the world through their sensitive lens. I have worked with so many sensitive little ones, but my experiences as a parent have given me a greater level of understanding of the depth of their feelings – and a greater level of empathy for parents who may be experiencing this depth of feeling for the first time.

I wish that I had a magic wand to conjure up a village for every family out there, but in the meantime I will do my best to empower you as a parent. My goal is to take you through the mind of a sensitive child, while also providing you with some tools to help these incredible little people flourish. While there are challenges that go hand in hand with feeling so much, there are also many strengths. Sensitive people often have high levels of empathy, which helps them connect with others and understand people's thoughts and feelings. They often have an appreciation of the beauty in the world and tend to be very creative once they find their passions and interests. Several studies have shown that these children develop great social skills (in time!) and really thrive in the right environment. I believe that when we understand the mind of a sensitive child, parenting them can be a magical journey.

CHAPTER 1

Understanding your sensitive child

Ciara and Tony are the parents of a five-year-old girl called Amy. Amy is their youngest, and they would describe her as very different to her older siblings. They realised early on that parenting Amy was definitely not 'by the book'. Trying to hold boundaries or discipline Amy has always been challenging and leads to a shutdown from her or appears to cause her a lot of distress. Her siblings don't tend to have difficulty finishing school and then engaging in extracurricular activities, but Amy seems to need quiet time. Filling her diary with too much can lead to overstimulation and overwhelm. She covers her ears when she is tired if anyone speaks to her too loudly, and they notice that she seems to have a heightened response to sensory inputs, like noises and certain foods, and she is particular about her clothes.

> *Ciara and Tony say that she also has the biggest heart. She retreats into herself if she is in trouble because they know she tries so hard to 'be good'. Feeling like she has disappointed them seems to result in painful emotions like sadness and shame. She takes her time to settle into new situations and when meeting new people, but once you are let in to her inner world, you discover she is full of love and capable of forging deep friendships with peers.*

Aspects of this story may resonate with you. Perhaps you have a child who, like Amy, has difficulty with boundaries, finds transitions challenging or has a tendency to shut down when they are overwhelmed. Perhaps your child is extremely empathic, finds it hard to accept criticism or is sometimes described as 'strong-willed'. If so, this book will guide you through these challenges and offer support during the exciting adventure of raising a highly sensitive child!

What do we mean by sensitive?

Psychologist Dr Elaine Aron first coined the term 'high sensitivity' in 1996. Since then, thanks to so many pioneers in the field of research, like Professor Michael Pluess, it is now widely accepted that:

- Sensitivity is a continuum from low to average to high sensitivity, with 30 per cent of people classed as low, 40 per cent as medium and 30 per cent as high.

- Sensitivity is a result of our neurobiology, our evolution and our genetics.
- Sensitivity is impacted by both nature and nurture and is influenced by the environment and experiences across the lifespan.
- Highly sensitive people are more strongly impacted by stressful life experiences, particularly as children.
- Highly sensitive people tend to benefit more from positive experiences than people who are less sensitive.

One of the reasons it is so important to understand sensitivity is because we know that sensitive children are more impacted by their environment, for better and for worse. This means that, given the right conditions, they can really thrive. Unfortunately, it also means that sensitive children are more vulnerable to experiencing psychological pain due to their capacity to feel so much.

My favourite way of explaining this comes from the research by Professors Thomas Boyce and Bruce Ellis. We know that roughly 30 per cent of the population are 'dandelions', meaning they are sturdy, transplantable survivors who can grow and thrive in most environments. There are, of course, exceptions to this, especially when we think about childhood abuse and neglect. Another 30 per cent are 'orchids' – a much more delicate flower that needs a lot more nurturing to grow. If we mind these orchids delicately, planting them in warm, nurturing homes and schools, they have the capacity to flourish into the most resilient people. They tend to show very high levels of emotional intelligence, form deep and meaningful connections with people and have creative futures. And we have a middle group that have come to be known as 'tulips'. The tulips account for the remaining 40 per cent of the population and fall somewhere in the middle of the two ends of the sensitivity scale. They are not as hardy as the dandelions but not as delicate as the orchids. If this sounds confusing to you, think of sensitivity as a spectrum from low to high, with a cohort of people being somewhere in between.

I sometimes worry that highlighting research about how important it is for our orchid children to be handled more sensitively may just feel like another pressure added to parents' already overflowing load. I genuinely believe parenting is the hardest job there is, and I have nothing but admiration and compassion for every parent. So if you are reading this and worrying about your sensitive child and how you have been parenting, know that we can always repair these things at any age, and we are all always learning. There is no such thing as the perfect parent, and I hope you will feel more at ease about that as you read on. I struggle with parenting all the time too, and that is after years of training and psychological support!

Understanding your child's brain

There is an old view in psychology that children are born as blank slates and that our personalities are shaped by our environment. Although the environment certainly plays an important role, we now know that children come into this world with their own unique temperaments. This is not something that we need to fix or change, rather it is something that empowers us to understand who they are. Our temperament is a mix of biological, genetic and neurological components. This means we are all born with certain characteristics, and these characteristics are then influenced by our environment.

Some children will be born into the world as very easy-going. They will go with the flow and often slot easily into routines, schedules and life in general. They don't seem fazed by much and transition quite easily through developmental stages. Some children will be born 'on the move' and are very active from the beginning, their little nervous systems wired in a way that makes them more distractable and less willing to sit in one place for long! Some children come into this world with a heightened stress response and feel everything very intensely. These are often our sensitive kids who feel everything that little bit *more* and often need a lot of co-regulation from us to help them feel calm.

In case you are unfamiliar with the term 'co-regulation', I will explain. You have most likely heard the term 'self-regulation', which refers to our ability to soothe and calm our stress response. Think of the times you take a deep breath instead of saying the thing you might regret, the times you get yourself in the zone so you can focus on a task, the times you say no to the glass of wine when you need to be up early the next day, the times you are patient despite feeling frustrated and so on. These are all examples of your ability to regulate your emotional responses.

We are not born with the ability to do this. Little babies and small children learn this through repeated, consistent patterns of responsive interactions with their caregivers. In other words, the ability to self-regulate comes from this process of co-regulation. When children are experiencing a big emotion, their little stressed nervous system needs help to soothe and feel at ease. We have a phenomenal opportunity to help our children by letting them borrow our calm. Our regulated nervous system soothes their dysregulated nervous system through simple things like touch and warm hugs, our soothing voice, a gentle and understanding gaze, and the ability to just be with, rather than fix, emotions that are expressing themselves. It can be helpful for parents to know here that our goal is not to take the emotion away, but to meet it with a softness and a compassionate hold that helps it feel seen. Years of co-regulation wires our child's nervous system to do this for themselves as they grow and eventually leads to those helpful self-regulation skills we have as adults.

I am well aware this all sounds a lot easier on paper than in real life – believe me, I know! There is nothing more challenging than trying to do this for your child when you feel burnt out yourself and have nothing in the tank. Bear with me if that resonates with you – this book should help you feel more equipped as you read on. While we get plenty of practical parenting advice, we are often given little information about parenting children with more sensitive nervous systems, those who feel everything deeply. This often translates into big feelings and behaviours, as their sensory and emotional systems process their internal and external world. And this nervous system is not your fault or because of anything you are doing wrong!

You might reflect here for your child:

- Are they always on the move, or can they sit still for longer periods of time?

- Are they relaxed and easy-going if there are changes to their routine, or do they become upset and stressed?
- Are they usually described as happy-go-lucky and smiling, or are they naturally more thoughtful and serious?
- Do they dive right in to new activities or when meeting new people, or are they more cautious of strangers and new settings?
- Do they keep persevering even if they find something hard, or do they become easily frustrated and give up quickly?

Research conducted by Thomas and Chess found that children appear to broadly fit into three types of temperament, with some children being a combination of all three. (Of course, this is generalising a little, and all children are unique, but it can be a helpful guide to think about.) These temperament types are:

- Adaptable: children with more adaptable temperaments tend to be generally content, adapt well to change and have quite regular sleeping and eating habits. I remember watching with awe in baby-and-toddler groups as these calm little beings sat happily in their buggies, ate whatever food they were given and transitioned from activities with little to no protest!
- Intense: our more intense children are often feeling their emotions deeply, passionate in their wants and needs, very active, have difficulty with change and usually have quite irregular sleeping and eating habits. For example, trying to get my children dressed is an Olympic sport! Their sleeping and eating patterns are whatever the opposite of a routine is,

and they often make me feel exhausted just looking at them. I say this with huge amounts of love and as one tired mother!

- Slow to warm: these children may feel a little more hesitant when meeting new people or in unfamiliar situations. They take longer to feel at ease and comfortable in new settings. They like to pause and reflect before they dive in, and this is often due to having a brain and nervous system that processes information deeply (we will talk about this more in chapter five).

These natural traits (temperament) we are all born with are influenced by the world around us. Our temperament interacts with our physical, personal, social and cultural environment. Some temperaments and environments complement each other, and some can be more challenging. This compatibility of a child's temperament with their environment is what has been described by researchers Thomas and Chess as 'goodness of fit'. The goodness of fit concept suggests that parental approaches aligned with a child's temperament supports optimal development, while a mismatch can cause difficulties. The key here is knowing that sometimes we need to adjust our parenting style to help nurture our child's strengths. Research shows us that our children tend to have much more positive developmental outcomes when there is high goodness of fit.

To understand how our temperament and its interaction in relational environment might be important, let's have a look at Lucy's story.

> Lucy is a nine-year-old with a big bubbly personality and a kind heart. She feels her emotions deeply and as a result has quite intense reactions to her environment. She tends to have low frustration tolerance in response to unexpected situations or changes in routine. This manifests as a lot of reactivity and big emotional outbursts. Lucy's mother also has a big personality and is described by others as 'our fierce and fiery friend'. They are a force to be reckoned with, these two! Lucy's mother loves to go with the flow and often makes last-minute plans for their family. Lucy, however, likes to plan ahead and does not like unexpected changes to her day. Unfortunately, these temperament types tend to clash when they are not supported. Lucy's mother becomes agitated and frustrated with Lucy for her inflexibility. She describes herself as 'having a short fuse' and finds Lucy's behaviour difficult to manage. Lucy craves structure and routine and feels like everything is out of control. She feels misunderstood and is finding it harder and harder to regulate her emotions.

To understand the importance of our temperament and how it fits with the physical environment, we can explore Jack's story.

> Jack is an eleven-year-old who craves movement. He loves wrestling and has enjoyed any form of rough-and-tumble play since he was a toddler. He loves being outdoors and finds sitting still for long periods of time extremely difficult. Jack attends a school in the city centre that has very little

outdoor space. Their yard at break consists of a small concrete patch outside. While tight, there is just enough space to kick a football around with peers. Jack's school is an hour away by car or public transport, so he also spends an extra two hours a day sitting down and constrained. His classroom is small, so there is little room for him to walk up and down or give his body the movement it is craving. As a result of this, Jack feels agitated and frustrated in school. He is highly aware of his behaviour and is a very conscientious child. He keeps this agitation inside during school but has many meltdowns when he gets home. He then beats himself up over his behaviour and cannot understand why he feels so angry all of the time.

I encourage you to reflect on your temperament and your child's and see if there is any way you can adapt your approach or the environment to meet their needs. Lucy's mom might need support in understanding Lucy's temperament and why her big emotions are becoming harder to manage. She likely needs help to adjust her expectations of Lucy and support Lucy where she is at, understanding that establishing familiarity in her day is what helps her to feel safe. Lucy's mom might try planning her week in advance so she can give Lucy time to process any changes to their routine. I know this won't always be possible and life is full of unexpected changes, but communicating this clearly to Lucy will help her feel seen and understood.

Jack probably needs help in school to have more movement breaks, giving his body the tension release it so badly needs. His family and school may need to come together and think about ways in which Jack can feel more supported. He may need extra time outside, especially when he comes home from school, recognising that this is just as much of a priority as any homework. Arguably, it is much more important, as it will help him to feel regulated enough to learn.

Our modern world is not always the most helpful for our children. I know that is frustrating to hear when this is the world we live in, and we don't have another option – I really do understand. But I believe if a child is struggling in some way, we should examine the environment before we conclude there is something wrong with our child. It is fascinating how much more at ease children can feel when there is high goodness of fit at home, in school, at extracurricular activities and so on.

The role of temperament early on

It is very possible to have a sensitive child who is experiencing the world deeply but doesn't seem too reactive early on – many sensitive children present as quite settled babies or toddlers. But here I want to touch on another cohort: babies who are extremely sensitive to their environment from the beginning. Many of you reading this book will have older children, but I hope this might still resonate in some way. It is important to note here, too, that if you have a baby who is hard to soothe and who seems particularly unsettled, linking in with your GP, public health nurse or paediatrician is always a good idea to make sure they have no physical difficulties or pains that are not obvious to us.

Let's have a look at Lisa and Emily's experience:

Lisa is a new mom who has just given birth to a little girl, Emily. Lisa is a little taken aback at how difficult those first few days in the hospital are, wondering why Emily is crying so much and seems so unsettled. Telling herself this is probably just how newborns are, she keeps going and does her best to soothe her. She has read plenty of baby books and has learned that 'you must try to put your baby in their cot early on, so they don't become too dependent on you for comfort'. She tries her best to settle Emily in her cot to no avail. Emily seems to wake suddenly at any movement, notices immediately if she is alone and cries as loudly as her little lungs can manage until she finally settles in Lisa's arms.

Lisa starts to notice a creeping inner voice whispering 'you can't do this' in her ear. Sleep-deprived and exhausted, she starts to internalise this. She begins questioning herself and her capability as a parent. 'Why can't I soothe her? What am I doing wrong?' She receives well-meaning advice from family and friends who don't seem to understand. 'You just need to keep trying', 'it's obviously your milk', 'it must be the wrong formula', 'you need to just let her cry it out', 'you're coddling her too much – she's become too attached to you' and the list goes on.

Things seem to go from bad to worse when she tries to leave the house – Emily gets distressed in the car, seems to find the buggy uncomfortable and generally appears unhappy everywhere. Lisa reads online that water and baths can be soothing for children, but Emily seems petrified of the bath. Lisa wonders if it's the sound of running water, or if the lights in the bathroom might be too bright, but making those changes doesn't seem to help either. Being damp, cold, hungry or in pain seems to set off an internal alarm, and Emily goes from zero to a hundred in a matter of seconds.

Lisa has tried a holistic approach in figuring out if there are any underlying causes. She visits doctors, osteopaths and craniosacral therapists with little ease in her daughter's distress. Despite each of these clinicians being helpful, there does not appear to be anything physiologically wrong with Emily. Lisa does everything possible to help Emily feel more at ease and is attuned to her needs as much as possible. When this does not appear to help Emily, Lisa concludes that the only explanation is her. She is failing as a mother. How do her friends seem to take parenthood in their stride, while internally she feels broken? She withdraws from friends because she feels like Emily's behaviour is a reflection on her and she can't cope with feeling judged. She is already judging herself enough.

Finally, Lisa meets a friend who mirrors her exact parenting journey. She breathes a sigh of relief when her friend tells her what she has learned about sensitive babies and how normal (whatever normal means) it is that these babies are reacting so strongly to their environment. Lisa learns that Emily has a sensitive nervous system and needs a lot more comforting to help her feel at ease. For example, now when Emily wakes in the night, Lisa no longer beats herself up that she has 'failed' but instead understands that Emily's little body and stress system just needs to be soothed and held. Lisa feels more confident to lean into soothing her daughter and reframes the challenges Emily is facing as understandable overwhelm in a new and scary world. She tells herself this will get easier and begins reaching out for support to friends and family.

This story is an amalgamation of many new parents I have worked with, along with my own personal journey. I am a sensitive person myself, and I have worked with many young people and adults who are sensitive souls, but I never knew what to expect in a sensitive baby. I am one of the lucky few who had access to information on this early on, so I very quickly realised it was not a reflection on me, but an amazing little person who was feeling everything so intensely.

So many parents I meet have not been given this information, and nearly all of them have experienced huge amounts of self-blame and shame, believing they are failing in some way. The lack of education available to parents on this is dangerous, as it can be a major factor in perinatal mental health challenges. The impact of feeling stressed and overwhelmed while trying to soothe a baby who is hard to soothe is excruciating. Early intervention saves lives and recognising these patterns is so important. It feels hard because it *is* hard, not because you have failed.

We will keep reflecting on stories related to each developmental stage as this book progresses. And while not every sensitive baby will be hard to soothe, I hope this provides you with some comfort if you have had that experience. I also hope it is becoming clear that, even from the beginning, these sensitive souls come into this world with their own unique temperament, and this is not your fault. I want us to remain hopeful because these children really are a gift. Although they make parenting more challenging, they bring so much joy and love into our lives too.

A deeper dive into sensitivity

To get a clearer picture of what sensitivity is, let's look at DOES, an acronym formulated by Dr Elaine Aron to distil the main characteristics of sensitivity.

D – DEPTH OF PROCESSING

A sensitive person's brain continues to process information when they have been exposed to something emotional far longer than others. This means that highly sensitive children tend to think about and process information on a deeper level than their less-sensitive peers. They are also noticing and taking in so much from their environment, always relating and comparing what they notice to their past experiences.

Have you ever wondered why your child surveys the room before running into a new environment? Why they might be initially more cautious, often mislabelled as 'shy'? Why they seem to get 'stuck' in bad moods sometimes? Why they might find it hard to move on from an argument? Why making decisions can be a stressful experience? Or why they seem to 'loop' with anxious thoughts over things they have said or done?

This is often as a result of this capacity for deep processing. It is an incredible gift in so many ways because it makes these children reflective and deep thinkers, but it can be hard to help them manage all of this. It can also feel quite frustrating for parents too, understandably!

I used to think I was a very anxious child. I would hate walking into a room first (I still do), and I always wished I could have a secret camera on an environment before I got there. Throughout primary school, I wondered why I found all of these seemingly 'normal' situations so stressful.

I now know this was not due (or at least not all due) to anxiety but because I wanted to know who would be there, where would be the comfortable place to sit, what the lighting would be like, how loud it would be, if there would be big crowds. I am an extravert, so I love being around people, but it always takes me a little while to settle in to a new environment, conversation or place. My mind is rushing with noticing all the subtleties happening because my brain is processing so much information.

O – OVERSTIMULATION

It makes sense that, given all of that deep processing going on, the little sensitive mind can become overwhelmed. Such deep reflective thinking is tiring for any nervous system, but it can be especially so for the developing brain. If your child is noticing every little thing, if the situation is complicated (lots of new skills to master, things to remember, a busy environment), intense (a lot of noise, lots of people, trying to concentrate in class) or lasts long in duration (travelling, playschool or school), it is likely to exhaust a sensitive child.

This is often evident after a day at school. The sensitive child has been concentrating all day, noticing the subtleties in the classroom, trying their best to regulate themselves, processing everyone's moods, their teachers' emotions, any difficulties with friends, breaktimes and so on. They come home then and most likely feel very overstimulated from the day. This might mean they need time alone to read or watch their favourite show, or maybe they just want to lie down.

It's helpful for parents to be attuned to this and set up the environment in a way that will help to reduce some of this overwhelm, though it's understandable that you might feel frustrated that they won't engage in conversation, seem to be really agitated and moody or seem to be having lots of meltdowns when they come home. In these situations, we can try to teach them what is happening in their little nervous systems and then have dedicated time for them to relax before engaging in homework or other activities.

Something I find fascinating about this is that some of us can keep going and going because our nervous system is loving all of the 'busyness'. We don't necessarily notice that we are becoming overwhelmed, and then by the time we do it's too late and we have a big crash in energy. I love being social and talking to friends, but I tend to hit a wall at a certain point, where any conversation after that involves huge amounts of effort and energy.

The same thing happens with our more sensory-seeking sensitive children. Often, we need to help them recognise they need to take a little break, spend some time allowing their nervous system to come back into balance and recharge.

E – EMOTIONAL REACTIVITY AND EMPATHY

Sensitive children experience their emotions deeply. This has a lot of benefits, as they tend to react more strongly to positive experiences than their less-sensitive peers. So if something good happens to them or to someone they care about, they will experience high levels of joy in response. But it can be challenging too, as they also experience greater emotional reactivity to less helpful situations and are impacted more deeply by them. This means that if something goes wrong or they feel sadness, shame or fear, they usually experience these emotions on a very deep level. This can be difficult to help them with, and I will talk more about this later (see chapter eight).

These children have very big hearts. This is not always as evident early on, when their little emotional brains are so reactive and pushing you to your limits! But as they grow, we see it emerging more and more. One reason for this is that sensitive people have increased activation in areas of the brain called the insula and the mirror neuron system, which are associated with awareness, integration of sensory information, empathy and action planning. Research has shown that the neurons of a sensitive person closely mirror the neurons of people they are watching do something or feel something. You might have noticed your child seems to be highly attuned to your emotions and moods – this can be hard on parents if they are feeling sad or struggling in some way and their child's antenna picks up on this. I often see my son watch me from the corner of his eye when I am sad about something, tentatively asking, 'You're sad, Mommy? Are you okay?' Some parents feel guilty about this and worry they are hurting their children in some way by exposing them to their emotions. I will explore this more as the book progresses but for now, just know that this is okay. We have a fantastic opportunity to model the healthy expression of difficult emotions for these children and show them how we help ourselves deal with them too.

S – SENSING THE SUBTLETIES

We are all born with a nervous system that is wired to keep us safe. So from the moment we are born, our little amygdala, where our fight/flight/freeze/fawn response is located, is scanning its environment to detect cues of threat and cues of safety. This is a process called neuroception (a term first introduced by Dr Stephen Porges, the developer of Polyvagal Theory). It is how we interpret our world for survival. For our more sensitive children, their nervous system is so finely tuned that they may be more likely to detect danger cues than others. This is one of the most helpful things to understand about these children and empower us to understand them.

Interoception is the process of perceiving and making sense of our internal world. It is how we process information about our internal state such as hunger, thirst, pain, temperature and our emotions. Our sensitive children are often sensory sensitive, meaning they often have a heightened awareness of these bodily signals and emotions. They interpret these signals intensely and as a result may be more overwhelmed by emotions and bodily sensations, activating their threat response. For example, feeling cold or hungry or being in pain is often experienced as very distressing, particularly during the younger years before they can put words on their experience. Sensitive babies are often a lot harder to soothe as not only are they experiencing their emotions strongly, but the physical feeling of being in pain, hungry and so on is also experienced deeply.

They also tend to be really impacted by their outer environment, so lights might be too bright, clothes too itchy, noises too loud, certain smells might be aversive and so on. This is called exteroception, which is the process of perceiving and making sense of our external world. It is how we process information from our external environment such as sight, touch, sound, taste and smell. These external sensations are often felt more deeply. They are not exaggerating when they say the sun is 'too sunny' or their clothes are itchy: this is being experienced in their nervous system to a heightened level. As a result of taking in so many subtleties from their outer world, it makes sense that it often takes sensitive children longer to feel comfortable or safe in a new environment or with new people.

Sensitivity and neurodivergence

The concept of neurodivergence is such a fascinating topic and I am excited to see so much more awareness being created about different neurotypes in both the mainstream media and in the scientific community. This is so important for equality, inclusion, acceptance and understanding. We live in a world that is set up for a 'neurotypical' brain, and unfortunately anything outside of that tends to be pathologised as it is different from the 'norm'. Thankfully, this is beginning to change thanks to so many brave neurodivergent voices and neuroaffirmative clinicians advocating for the minority.

I am privileged to be working therapeutically with both adults and children who have brains that work differently to a large proportion of the population (neurodivergent). Some of these children are highly sensitive, and some have defining features of other forms of neurodivergence including ADHD, autism and giftedness. There is currently no clear consensus in the literature about whether or not high sensitivity fits in this category. We still have so much to learn, and it is a definition that is continuing to evolve.

If we think about all forms of neurodivergence – such as autism, ADHD, giftedness and so on – in a Venn diagram, many of the features of sensitivity (sensory sensitivity, emotion reactivity, deep-processing brain, slow to warm, sensitive to overwhelm) can be overlapping features between them. The difference between high sensitivity and these other forms of neurodivergence is that they encompass features of a distinct brain style beyond sensitivity alone. This means that while sensitivity is often a feature of these beautiful brain styles, not all highly sensitive children will have defining features of these other forms of neurodivergence.

Unfortunately, the term 'highly sensitive' has come under scrutiny from some of the neurodivergent community. There is a concern that identifying with the trait of high sensitivity may lead to a missed diagnosis of other forms of neurodivergence

– meaning a parent may believe their child is 'just sensitive' and as a result will not seek the support or accommodations their child really needs. Their child may also lose access to a community that can help them feel seen and understood. I understand this concern and it is something I worry about too when creating awareness about highly sensitive children. For this reason, I always encourage parents to reach out for an assessment with a psychologist if they have any wonderings around this. Sometimes we worry about labels and diagnoses, but I wholeheartedly believe that learning about ourselves and the way our brains and nervous systems are wired is one of the most empowering things we can do for both ourselves and our children.

The reality is that we all present differently in the world, and we have attributes and traits that are similar to those of various unique and fantastic brains, whether those brains are 'neurotypical' (whatever that really is for any of us!) or neurodivergent or somewhere in between. I work with many young children and adults across many spectrums, and the one thing I learn more every day is that, while there are differences, we are all far more alike than we realise.

Whether our child is sensitive, autistic, gifted or so on, the approach we take in parenting them will be similar. We want most of all to help our children feel understood, validated and loved for who they are deep down. We want them to feel accepted and empowered in whatever way their wonderful selves are wired.

A quote I love that really encapsulates this chapter is by Alexander Den Heijer: 'When a flower doesn't bloom, you fix the environment in which it grows, not the flower.'

CHAPTER 2

Your child's window of tolerance

The idea of a 'window of tolerance', coined by Dr Dan Siegal, can help us to understand a sensitive nervous system. We all have a certain window in which we can manage a range of experiences and sensations throughout our day. When we are operating within our window, we feel regulated and able to manage stressors that might arise. We have access to our thinking, rational brain that helps us to think, feel and behave in ways that help to keep us grounded and able to cope with the difficulties life throws at us.

When you are at ease and feel connected to your wise self, this is usually a good indicator that you are operating within your window of tolerance. It might be helpful to pause now and reflect on what your body language and facial expressions look like when you feel like this. This is called the 'optimal zone' of arousal, where we feel our most centred and connected to ourselves – it's also referred to as our 'comfort zone'.

How much space we have in our window on any given day depends on numerous factors. The pain of struggling with relationship difficulties, physical illnesses, grief, loss, financial stress or other social and emotional difficulties will all, understandably, narrow our window. Childhood adversity and trauma also influence how this window develops and how sensitive it can be to stress. Physiological states that are difficult to manage, like sensory overwhelm, thirst, hunger, tiredness and so on, can also narrow our window throughout the day.

When we become stressed or overwhelmed, we can be pushed out of our windows more easily. It is helpful to understand this in ourselves and our children so that we can spot the signs and know how to help. We can probably all relate to feeling anxious, agitated and irritated. This is usually a warning sign that we are being pushed up into what is called 'hyperarousal'. When we get tipped too far out of our window and further into hyperarousal, we can feel extremely anxious, out of control or angry. Our fight/flight reactions are often activated, and we want to fight or run away. Our thoughts are usually racing, our breathing is shallow, and we experience a lot of adrenaline and cortisol.

Sometimes we get pushed down out of our window into what is called 'hypoarousal'. The initial warning signs may be that we start to feel very low or like we are shutting down. We might notice our energy dips and our body starts to feel heavy. We often feel cold and tired. We might feel a bit 'zoned out' or spacy. When we get tipped further into hypoarousal, we can feel completely numb and detached from our emotions. Our body has gone into a state of freeze, and people often feel 'outside of themselves'. Hyper- and hypoarousal are both adaptive coping responses that are generally outside of our conscious control.

We can all take steps to widen our windows and come back into our optimal zones, but we often need a little help and guidance with this.

The early years

The parents I work with find the window of tolerance a helpful way of understanding why their child seems to become so quickly activated under stress. Deep-feeling, sensitive souls are born into this world with heightened emotional awareness. As a result of feeling so deeply, they can be pushed out of their window of tolerance more easily. This is nothing to fear and is just due to their temperament and the way their brain and nervous system is wired. It is a great thing, in many ways, as although they can be more easily overwhelmed, they also experience excitement and joy with just as powerful a force. They are responding and reacting to their experience with more heightened awareness than a child who is not so sensitive. It makes sense that their threat system may become more easily activated, and we can help them with this through the process of empathy and connection.

Many factors influence this window of tolerance for our sensitive children early on. One example that is often overlooked is how a traumatic birth or a NICU stay can influence how heightened their stress response is from the beginning. Their window of tolerance for managing intense emotions may understandably be a little smaller due to early life stress they experienced. This will not impact every child in the same way, as they are all unique, but it might help to reflect on Kelly's story.

> *Kelly is a new mother who has recently given birth to a little boy, Noah. Unfortunately, Kelly developed sepsis after Noah was born, when a strep B infection went undetected during a screening exam. Thankfully, Kelly was okay, and Noah was showing no signs of infection, but he was given six days of antibiotics as a precautionary measure. This meant Noah needed a lumbar puncture, which involves a small needle being inserted into the lower back to test a sample of cerebrospinal fluid for any possible infections, along with a cannula, which is a little tube, inserted in his hand for his IV antibiotic. It sounds pretty scary, but the clinicians involved are very skilled and do it so quickly and gently that many babies barely notice.*
>
> *Noah was not one of these babies. Being a sensitive little soul on high alert already, he found this extremely distressing. He wanted to be close to his mom and, despite nursing staff being incredibly nurturing towards him, he would cry as loudly as his little lungs could manage every time he was taken away for his infusions. He was visibly distressed every time he noticed the cannula that was hurting his little hand. Kelly saw how he would cling to her with all his might and how scared he was when he experienced any separation from her. She watched other*

new mothers changing their babies' nappies with ease while Noah screamed with fear each time he was put down.

Something this story helps us reflect on is that 'trauma is not what happens to you, trauma is what happens inside you as a result of what happens to you' (Dr Gabor Maté). Two people or two babies could go through the same event and experience it completely differently. For one, the situation could be moderately stressful. For the other, depending on how sensitive their nervous system is, it could be experienced as traumatic. Something that can be so confusing for parents is why their baby appears to be so stressed following birth trauma when they surely can't remember it.

Implicit memories begin forming when a baby is in the womb. Before the age of one and a half, they are the only memories a child has access to. These memories might be the comfort of being cuddled, the regulating feeling of being rocked, the sensation of warm milk, caregivers' smiles and sounds.

Trauma-related implicit memories are not available to our conscious mind, but that doesn't mean we don't carry them with us. Just as our children encode feelings of safety and security in implicit memory, they also encode anything that is scary for them. So although they can't recall being born or NICU stays, these memories are stored in their emotional brain and may impact them in certain ways – meaning that while they might not consciously remember, their bodies do. This might mean it takes longer for them to realise they are safe when the scary event is over. They might react to things they don't understand like nappy changes, being undressed, being washed, as if the frightening event is happening again. This can be so hard for parents to manage as you are left wondering what you are doing wrong and why your baby seems so hard to soothe. Recognising early on that their child's window of tolerance is smaller often helps parents feel less stressed and less like they are failing. However, I also always advocate for any parent who is worrying about their child or struggling to please link in with their GP, public health nurse or paediatrician. Trying to persevere while feeling unsure, distressed or overwhelmed can be incredibly stressful. Please don't suffer in silence and reach out for support if you need it. A list of support services is included at the back of this book.

Whether or not our babies underwent stressful early experiences, we know that our more sensitive children have a more sensitive nervous system and are experiencing their world deeply. This means that these babies need a lot of soothing and comforting to help calm their physiology. They are often the babies who will only settle in our arms and who seem to follow a different rhythm to a baby with a more easy-going temperament. If we think back to Kelly's story, it would be empowering for her to know that Noah is likely going to be on higher alert than if that had not been his start in life. It would be so helpful for Kelly to know that this is nothing to fear, and that Noah will be fine – he just needs time to realise the threatening event is over. Lots of cuddles and responding to his upset by holding, rocking, swaying, gently humming and using a soothing tone of voice should help wire Noah's nervous system for safety over time. Holding them close and attending to them when they are upset helps wire their brain for safety and security and soothes their little fight/flight response. And please remember, you could be doing everything 'perfectly', but these children often just take a little longer to feel at ease in the world.

Sleep

My introduction to motherhood was with the most amazing little guy who would not and could not sleep anywhere but my arms. I, like many other new parents, had internalised the idea that this was somehow not okay. I had heard that babies should be in their own room after six months and that you need to put them asleep in their cots. Then along came my Velcro baby and I really felt like I was failing in some way. I kept trying to put him down 'drowsy but awake', as the saying goes, and all I ever saw were two huge wide eyes staring back at me as if to say, 'What do you think you are doing?' A little alarm would set off in his fight/flight response as he realised he was apart from me, and this would lead to a lot of upset until he was back in his safe place.

I am talking about babies here, but sleep tends to be a challenge for sensitive children throughout their younger years, as they often seek more reassurance and connection to help their emotional brain feel safe enough to rest. While some children seem to come into this world as great sleepers, others unfortunately don't, so expectations around sleep can cause added stress to parents who are already exhausted.

I am always sad to see this pathologised in the literature or even among clinicians. I have seen articles stating that a parent who continues supporting their child to sleep as they get older is doing this due to their own anxiety and an anxious attachment between the parent and child. This is disheartening to read when we have so much research on temperament and how some children need a little more support from their parent to help them feel safe. It is perfectly normal for some children to seek more connection and soothing. They may want more hugs, more closeness and more holding, and that is not something we need to fear or pathologise. It is also potentially harmful messaging for any parent who is trying to do the best they can to support their child but begins to internalise their child's sleep as a reflection on them. As a culture, we should ask ourselves why we view responding to our child in times of stress or fear as a negative thing. Of course we want to promote independence in our children, and yes, depending on the attachment relationship of the parent and child, there may be times when the parent's anxiety is a contributing factor. But for a huge proportion of our sensitive children, this biological need for comfort and connection continues after baby- and toddlerhood, and often particularly around the long separation of night-time. Independence stems from dependence and from repeated instances of feeling safe, loved and supported.

The reality is that some children need lots of co-regulation at night to help them feel safe: our calming presence beside them helps their little body and nervous system feel soothed. For some, it may mean they want to tuck in beside us, our scent, touch and body heat helping them feel at ease. For others, it may be simply knowing they are not alone in their room and that we are there if they need us.

Some popular publications on babies and sleep highlight that babies need to learn how to self-soothe. However, young children acquire the skills to soothe themselves in response to how they are soothed by their caregivers. So while some may settle themselves back asleep, they are not actually self-soothing. When we hear that fight/flight cry (it often sounds like an angry cry) then they are seeking comfort, connection and safety and, if possible, we should respond to them. The science on brain development tells us that, ideally, we should not leave them in high-stress states for long periods of time. Self-soothing is not actually possible from a developmental perspective, and child development experts suggest that it is more likely babies who have been left to cry have become so stressed that they have shut down. A related study found that while these babies may not cry out anymore, their cortisol (stress) levels continue to remain high. This means that, while they are not outwardly signalling for help, internally they are experiencing stress. How much this will impact each child is individual and often comes down to their window of tolerance and their temperament. Ideally, the moments our children are crying at night are the times we continue to provide them with reassurance and safety, fostering their sense of trust in us.

Something that unfortunately isn't normalised in western society is that small children are hardwired to be close to us. It's completely normal for them to want to be close to their parents, and there is no exact time by which a baby or toddler 'should' be sleeping through the night! There are so many reasons why they might wake – they might feel lonely, scared, a new baby has arrived, their teeth hurt, they have a cold and so on. There is also no exact time by which they 'should' be in their own room. Our beliefs about sleep are more a reflection of the culture we live in rather than of the research and developments in science. Western society promotes independence early on, and we tend to judge others who sleep with their children. It is viewed as strange in a culture that promotes individualism. However, the majority of non-western societies co-sleep and have been co-sleeping for thousands of years. Research by Professor James McKenna has, in fact, shown that when parents and babies sleep together, their heart rates, brainwaves, sleep states, oxygen levels, temperatures and breathing influence one another. The research shows that when parents and babies sleep together, while they might wake more frequently, they actually sleep longer overall. This is often because parents don't have to get out of bed to settle the child if they are hungry, looking for a soother and so on. These parents may co-sleep by sharing the same room, with their child sleeping on a separate surface, or they may bedshare, meaning they sleep on the same surface as their child. There are important risks to consider if you do this too and following the 'safe sleep seven' is so important (see further resources for details).

You might be reading this and thinking, 'No thanks, Aoife, I need my sleep!' And that is so understandable. This is not for every family, and it certainly doesn't mean those who don't co-sleep are creating anxious children! It is just helpful for those who do to know they are doing nothing wrong, and it serves as a reminder that it is biologically very normal.

SLEEP TRAINING
Something I worry about when writing about sleep is that parents may feel ashamed if they sleep train their children. While it is

important to know what is optimal in meeting a baby's need for comfort, safety and soothing, sometimes doing this is not always possible.

I work with a huge cohort of parents who are completely burnt out and exhausted. Trying to meet the demands of parenting can often (quite rightly) feel like it's all too much. Many parents are also experiencing the pain of struggling with mental health difficulties themselves. Sleep, or should I say the lack of, is significantly impacting their ability to function and be present during the day. They are trying their very best to put one foot in front of the other, and not having enough rest is contributing to their ability to take care of themselves. This then makes it feel even more challenging to take care of their baby. While I believe parents should be empowered and supported in meeting their baby's needs, the reality is that when a parent is really struggling, taking care of their mental health should always take priority. I have sadly worked with too many parents who have pushed themselves beyond their capacity and the result has been a rapid decline in their functioning along with high levels of anxiety and stress. It is vital that parents are empowered in recognising just how important it is to take care of themselves too so that they can be emotionally and physically resourced enough to take care of their child.

Many parents I work with have tried their best to be as responsive as possible at night only to realise it still feels 'too hard and too much'. This is not a reflection of how much these parents love their children, but more indicative of their support systems and how much they have in their window of tolerance at the time. In this case, the best decision they made for their family and for their mental health was to sleep train their child. The decision to do this is often more nuanced than it seems. It is also so important to say that not all sleep training methods involve the 'cry it out' approaches and that there are many more gentle sleep training methods that do their best to minimise the stress and upset for the child. Another important research finding is that for 20 per cent of children (that is quite a lot, 1 in 5) no form of sleep training appears to work. This is key information for any parent who is already struggling and starts to internalise 'I can't even get sleep training right; I am a failure'. There are often underlying factors such as developmental differences, temperament, and medical reasons (reflux, physiological pain) why a child is struggling with sleep. Please do reach out to your paediatrician for support if you have any concerns.

I firmly stand by the belief that we should never judge another until we have walked in their shoes. So please be kind to yourself for the decisions you make around this and know that there are many ways we can continue to develop nurturing connections with our children and repair. Every family has to do what works for them as a whole.

Transitions

For our more sensitive children, transitions can sometimes be a challenge. Some examples of transitions are moving from ending the weekend to starting the new week, getting up in the morning to getting dressed, playing to having breakfast, watching television to doing homework or travelling from school to home.

You will probably hear me repeat this a few times in this book, but it is helpful to know that, where possible, sensitive children often need us to go a little slower with transitions and remind ourselves that they often just need a bit more time. This is hard for parents because our schedules are busy, and taking our time isn't always practical or realistic. This means sometimes we have to rush children when it might be more helpful to go slowly, or we have no choice but to leave them somewhere when, ideally, we would take more time to help them settle, or for whatever example we think of, despite our best efforts, we just don't have the resources or time! And on top of all of that, trying to help them when they are overwhelmed and their nervous system is stressed tests the most patient caregiver out there. Let's have a look at Ava's story to illustrate some of this.

Ava is a kind-hearted, sensitive seven-year-old with a loving family who want the best for her. She is the youngest of three siblings, and because of the way her nervous system is wired, she has always needed that little bit more care. Her parents have managed this as best they could but currently feel exhausted and burnt out trying to manage transitions.

Getting Ava to school in the morning can be really difficult and is beginning to cause distress for the whole family. Her parents notice that, no matter how much sleep she has had the night before, she wakes up in the morning most days quite upset. Feeling rushed and under time pressure appears to set off an alarm in her fight/flight

> *response. This translates to Ava shouting and refusing to get up, screaming at everyone to leave her alone and lots of big emotions.*
>
> *Ava's parents report feeling extremely upset by this, as they can see the impact it has on her, but they have two other children to get ready for school too, and they don't have the resources or time to help her. They both have busy jobs and feeling so stressed themselves every morning is taking a toll on their mental health. They have tried everything from being compassionate and understanding to a more punitive approach that results in consequences for her behaviour, but nothing seems to be helping. This all results in having to force Ava up, get her dressed and, mid-meltdown, put her in the car for school. They find this difficult to understand because Ava loves school. She has many friends and has a great relationship with her teacher. Like all children, she needs little breaks now and again, but for the most part school is a happy place for her.*

If we remember that these children often just need a little more time (as understandably hard as this can be on parents sometimes) then we might dissect the morning routine a little more closely.

> *Ava can find it hard to fall asleep as that deep-processing brain of hers reflects on her day, thoughts swirling around, and it takes time for her to slow down and sleep. She is often quite tired in the morning as her little mind is so*

busy, and waking up and being rushed can push her out of her window of tolerance. Waking up releases adrenaline and cortisol into our system that kick our body into action. Because a sensitive child experiences their emotions more deeply, waking can be particularly hard, as their body feels this rush of stress hormones as quite stressful. Add in the anxiety and hurrying that happen for us all, and that little alarm in Ava's limbic system might start firing. Her emotion centres feel like they are under attack, and as a result her behaviour becomes that of attacking energy. So she begins screaming, kicking, refusing to get up and internally feels flooded with anger and distress.

One thing that might help Ava is a slower transition for her in the morning. Every child is different, so what helps Ava might not necessarily work for someone else, but hopefully these ideas might guide your thinking. Now, her parents begin setting their alarm 20 minutes earlier. Every morning they go in and lie beside Ava, gently rousing her and letting her know it's the morning but that there is no rush to get up. They buy a little lava lamp to keep beside her bed that Ava finds very regulating to look at in the morning. They give her deep-pressure hugs and rub her head for a few minutes as she slowly wakes up a little more. A 'cosy morning' awaits her downstairs, where her favourite breakfast is laid out. There is no pressure to get into her uniform until after breakfast, and cosy PJs and slippers are the new breakfast attire. Ava loves the piano, so rather than putting on the radio, the speakers play soft piano background

> music as a calming regulatory sound while they have their breakfast. *This slight change in routine in the morning helped the family as a whole, as Ava feels much more regulated and therefore has a lot less emotion overflow.*

I realise that this requires a lot of patience, and it won't always be practical, but when possible, slight changes on our end can make transitions much easier for us all. If your child is struggling with any transition, it can be helpful to keep reminding yourself to go slowly and, if you can, give them more time.

One concern parents often have here is 'Aoife, that's just not real life! The world is not set up in this way, and she has to learn how to adjust. Life won't coddle her like this.' And you're right. The world is not set up for our children who need a little more time. What we often don't realise, though, is the more we help them with the things we can control, the easier it is for them to handle the things we can't control. We worry about life not being helpful, so we mirror that and hope we can teach them out of the difficulties they are having. But we don't necessarily take their developmental stage into account when we think about this – just because they are finding something challenging now, it doesn't mean they will always find it so.

With the right adjustments and support, they can begin to learn how to help themselves as they grow. For example, Ava might understand as a teenager that she needs a little more time in the morning to prepare herself for secondary school. She knows to set her own alarm earlier, to have her clothes ready so she's not rushed and stressed and so on.

TALKING YOUR CHILD THROUGH TRANSITIONS

When we help our children to figure out how to mind their nervous system, especially how to tune into what they need most during moments of overwhelm and dysregulation, their brain begins to wire itself in a way that makes it easier for them to access those regulatory systems when they are alone. We can do this by spending some time helping them to understand the *why* behind their big feelings. These children often feel guilty and ashamed of their actions. They can be just as confused as others when they feel overcome by their emotions and act in ways that are not always helpful. Here is an example of how you could help them understand this – you know your child best, so feel free to just use this as a guide and change any language you want to!

> I wanted us to sit and have a chat about something that I love about you so much. Do you know that you have a really cool brain? It's so special because it can often see things and notice things that some of us miss. This cool brain can think really deeply and feel emotions really deeply too. This is an amazing superpower, and it is what helps you see all the magic in the world!
>
> What can be a bit hard is that, because this cool brain can think and feel so much, sometimes it can get a little fuzzy and feel a little stressed. This makes perfect sense because it's so busy and working so hard all the time – this happens to us adults too! Sometimes when this happens our feelings get really big, and they often fly out through our bodies. That's why we all shout

sometimes or feel like throwing things sometimes. The great news is that we can learn how to manage this so that our fuzzy brains don't take over all the time. I will always help you with this.

What do we do and how do we help?

To help sensitive children learn how to regulate their emotions, it's useful to first understand the neuroscience behind the behaviour. Understanding a child's brain can help us hugely when their nervous systems are activated, and we feel stressed.

Sometimes we try to help children by using a top-down approach that focuses on trying to reason with them. Have you ever tried to reason with your child when they are having a meltdown by telling them to use their words or to calm down? We feel understandably frustrated, and we try to talk to them; we ask them to use their words or tell us what's wrong. We tell them to calm down and try to meet them on a cognitive level. I have done this many times and it rarely helps. Think about how you feel when someone tells you to calm down or asks you to explain yourself in the moment. We all do this to each other from time to time, and although we mean well when we tell others to calm down or to talk to us rationally, it often only escalates the behaviour. The reason being able to calm down is so hard in a situation like this is that we don't have access to the area of our brain that helps us to do this when we are dysregulated.

Our brains develop from the bottom up, starting with our brainstem (our survival brain) and ending with the cortex, our thinking, rational brain. In order to use top-down approaches (e.g. talking, trying to rationalise) when we are stressed, we need to have a very organised cortex – this area of the brain is still developing into our late twenties. Some of us (myself included) have a cortex that is quite sensitive; this means it can be extremely hard to access our thinking, rational brain when we feel overwhelmed. Many things can impact how robust our cortex is, including childhood trauma, experiencing bullying growing up, chronic stress, physical illness and being from a marginalised population. The research shows us that even if a cortex is well developed, its functioning drops to 10 per cent capacity when we are under a lot of stress. The lower parts of our brain become overwhelmed, and we have very limited access to our thinking, rational brain. So you can see how complex this really is, especially for children with more sensitive nervous systems.

If you are interested in reading more about this, I highly recommend reading the work of Dr Bruce Perry. He is a pioneering neuroscientist in the field of trauma and has done incredible research that highlights that in order to help a child learn, think and reflect on their behaviour, we need to intervene in a simple sequence. This sequence is called the Three Rs.

THE THREE RS: REACHING THE LEARNING BRAIN

1. REGULATE

The first thing we do is regulate our own emotions. This can be hard to do when we feel really stressed. A screaming baby, a toddler or a child of any age having a meltdown is distressing. Our own fight/flight/freeze/fawn reactions get triggered, and we can feel upset, frustrated and angry. When this happens, just know it is easier to access the regulatory networks in our brain by targeting our brainstem (the lower region of our brain) rather than trying to reason with our cortex. In order to do this, and soothe our nervous system, we can follow a few steps.

The first step is recognising that we feel overwhelmed. I know that sounds easy, but it is actually a skill and a practice that takes time to learn, especially during these intense moments when we are flooded with emotion. The second step might sound a bit cliché, but never underestimate the power of the breath! There is a reason we hear this advice so much – it really is one of the fastest ways of helping us regulate. Practise taking a few deep breaths slowly: breathe in, hold for a few seconds and then an even longer exhale. If you are unsure how to do this, it might be helpful to imagine doing a few big sighs! This activates our parasympathetic nervous system and helps our body relax. The third step is validating our own emotions. Many of us feel annoyed with ourselves for reacting, and we are not good at being compassionate towards ourselves and acknowledging how challenging all of this is. We can practise using a mantra like: 'You're okay. It's understandable you feel overwhelmed – this is so hard to listen to'. The fourth step is asking yourself: 'What do I need right now?' If we can create a little space for ourselves, that's great, but if not, what might help us cope in the moment? A phrase that helps me is: 'My child is having a hard time – they are not trying to give me a hard time.' I know it can be hard to remind ourselves of this, but it becomes easier the more we practise it!

Finally, we can begin activating our brainstem by engaging in something that is patterned, repetitive and rhythmic. This is where we can join forces with our child and model by using deep breathing together or rocking them in our arms as we sway the stress away. Humming can be particularly powerful in soothing an activated brain. It might sound strange but try it now as you are reading this and check in with how you feel! Dancing and music can be an excellent way of taking us out of our head and into our body. Some other ways to do this are jumping, drumming, tapping, bouncing on a trampoline, skipping. Anything that is patterned, repetitive and rhythmic will help us and our children regulate our emotions.

It is important to know that some children do not want our touch when they are dysregulated. Their sensory system may find touch overwhelming in these moments – these are the children who push us away if we try to hug them. We can always ask them if they would like a hug, and if they say no, we can be a supportive presence nearby, saying something like: 'I see you're having a hard time, love – I am here when you need me' in a soothing tone. We might take a few deep breaths ourselves and model for them that we are a calming presence beside them. You may find they are ready for hugs and touch when they have had a little bit of space.

One of my children screams ear-piercingly loudly when they are upset about something. His little face turns bright red and what comes out of his mouth is an angry roar! I am always fascinated to see how quickly this angry roar turns to tears when I respond with empathy and kindness. I know this is hard to do – we are all human and it's difficult to stay calm sometimes, but it really does get easier, I promise! Always remember it is usually the most explosive behaviours that have the most pain underneath.

Now that we have regulated our emotions, we can have a think about step two.

2. RELATE

Next, we relate and connect with our child through an attuned and sensitive relationship. This is important for our sensitive kids who tend to feel embarrassed or ashamed about their emotional outbursts. Our tone of voice can convey our empathy and understanding about what happened. Again, this is just my language so feel free to change this in a way that resonates with you, but an example might be:

> It's okay, love, I am here. I know you are feeling sad and angry about not being allowed to cycle to the park, that makes sense. It all built up inside and those big feelings flew out. When that happens, it is so hard to feel calm. That's okay – it happens to all of us. I remember when I was your age, and my mom wouldn't let me cycle my bike to the park either, and I felt angry and upset too. I am sorry you are feeling that way. I love you so much and I know you didn't mean to shout.

The more we relate to children, the more they can learn from their behaviour and feel safe enough with us to hear our feedback. This is something we all should remember in our relationships: we all act in ways that are unhelpful sometimes because we have been triggered by something. You might resonate with that awful feeling you get after you have said something you regret in the middle of an argument. It can be hard even as adults to understand why we do or say things we don't mean. The more we can show our children we 'get it', it helps them feel less ashamed and defensive in their interactions with us. It also helps them feel safe enough with us to begin to reflect on their behaviour. This brings us to the final step.

3. REASON

This is where we can help our child to reflect, learn, remember, articulate and feel self-assured. We can help them learn how to label their emotional experience by thinking through a little emotions wheel.

We can gently try to understand what happened and what emotion they are feeling in their body. Did someone say something that made them feel angry or upset? Did they feel left out, ignored, embarrassed, criticised? Was there too much going on – did they feel sensory overwhelm? In my case, at the moment, it's always wondering whether it is some kind of sibling challenge. Were they upset that they had to share their toys? Are they upset about not having as much one-on-one connection? If your child seems to have a trigger that sets off an emotion alarm, you can help them reflect on what thoughts were running through their mind. Maybe it was 'I hate you', 'I am so sick of this', 'You're so mean, no one understands' or something similar. We can help them understand what emotions feel like in our body. Anger often feels hot, our fists and jaw clench and so on.

We might say, 'Ah yes, looking at our wheel this all makes sense! I turned off the TV even though your favourite show wasn't finished. You felt hot inside and angry and thought, "This is so unfair." It sounds like those big feelings got so big that they flew out when you hit me. I get it. I'm sorry you got a fright when I turned the TV off, but it is never okay to hit me – okay, love? Hitting really hurts people. Let's put our heads together and think about what might help the next time that hot angry feeling comes up.'

You might be rolling your eyes on reading the above sentence, and I can't say I blame you! You might be thinking, 'Ah here, Aoife, this is a time for harsher discipline!' I know it sounds strange but please do bear with me. If we keep coming back to the premise that our children are acting mainly from their emotional brain and an underdeveloped ability for impulse control, it helps us understand a little more. The more we pause ourselves and imagine how it feels to be in their shoes, their behaviour often makes sense. You might think back to your childhood. Were there ever times your parents made abrupt decisions 'because I said so' that felt like the meanest thing in the world to you at the time? I wasn't allowed to rollerblade on our road when I was younger – and my parents were dead right to make this decision, considering we lived on a main road. It was a very wise decision from a safety perspective. However, my seven-year-old brain heard this communicated as 'no means no' as they did not expand on their reasoning for why I couldn't go, and I still remember how unjust and unfair this felt. It is not that we don't hold these boundaries, or we don't tell our children that their behaviour is not okay. It's just the way in which we do it might first and foremost empathise with their big feelings and reactions. Give this a go and see if anything changes for you. I am always amazed at how helpful this type of reasoning can be with our children. The biggest behaviours often learn how to soften when they are met with a gentle and understanding approach.

We can get really creative with our kids in thinking about what helps them regulate. Punching pillows, using stress balls, wrapping themselves in heavy blankets – the list goes on. This might sound like it only works for an older child, but we can begin modelling this gentle curiosity about emotions and behaviour from infancy. We can do this by narrating out loud whenever we act in ways that might be a little reactive, talking about our thoughts and feelings and why we reacted in such ways. Children as young as two and three begin internalising this reflective approach. I recently observed one of my children going into the corner to take a few deep breaths when he is feeling stressed – it is fascinating how quickly they can learn.

Similarly, please don't worry if you haven't been doing this! There is no perfect approach, and we can learn these skills at any age. The main thing is just leaning heavily on the relationship. You will hear me say this time and time again, but when our relationship with our children is strong, it makes it so much easier for them to learn. It is no surprise that a child who has a good relationship with their teacher is eager and willing to learn in that class. That is not necessarily because they love the subject, but rather they are intrinsically motivated to care about that dynamic because they care about the person and they feel safe with them. The same goes for us as adults: we are more likely to grow and accept feedback from someone who we know understands and loves us than from those whom we feel misunderstood or unheard by. My biggest piece of parenting advice is to try your best to let your child feel really seen by you. Even when their behaviour is confusing and you don't understand, let them know you are trying to and that they mean the world to you.

I wrote the poem below to help understand transitions through the eyes of a sensitive child. This poem is about a toddler, but it might help guide your thinking.

I Wish I Knew How to Tell You

I wake up sometimes and my heart feels heavy, yet I can't quite describe why.
Everything is changing lately, and I wonder why I cry.
So many new skills to master, so many uphill climbs.
New school, new people, you're back to work, our distance feeling strange.

I need you more at night again, as there are sometimes monsters in my dreams.
You feel so safe and warm to me, when the morning light creeps through the beams.
You don't seem to see me yet, as you blink through tired eyes.
And when you finally look right at me, you exhale slowly with a sigh.
I think again about emotions, and if you might be mad.
While a little lump gathers in my throat, and I realise that maybe I feel sad.

You smile at me and my face lights up, feeling excited about the day.
I look around for my favourite toys, hoping to engage you in my play.
Everything happens so quickly then, as you rush me to get dressed.
We're being hurried along for breakfast, and I feel a tightness across my chest.

I want to make you happy, but I don't like that toothbrush near my face.
I run from my jacket and shoes, as a last attempt to stay in my safe place.
Your voice is louder now, that gentle voice sounds stressed.
I hear your frustration, and how much you need to rest.

My body moves in ways that feel outside of my control.
Pushing, flailing, kicking and I see the confusion on your face.
My head feels hot and it's hard to breathe, as I know I'm running out of time.
My ears ring from the fright of something loud, before I realise that noise was mine.

I wish I knew how to tell you that transitions can feel stressful.
It's hard for me to process how quickly the world seems to move.
I do also sometimes wonder if you forget I'm only two.
Please be patient and please be kind, I'll get there really soon.
I always just wish I had a little more time with you.

CHAPTER 3

Our own life history

You might be wondering why this chapter and the next one are about us, the parents, as this is a book about our children. Bear with me. The reason I feel so strongly about becoming more aware of ourselves is because having a child who feels deeply often evokes our own inner child and touches on our own inner-child wounding. This can leave us feeling overwhelmed by parenting and confused about our feelings and responses towards our children. I hope these chapters will help guide you towards an awareness of your own inner child and help you feel more compassionate towards yourself.

Your own window of tolerance

Before we begin, it is important to think about our own window of tolerance again and just how challenging it might be for you being either a sensitive parent or not-so-sensitive parent. Remind yourself that it is normal to find things hard and that neither way of being in the world is 'better' – they are just different. I, for one, am so thankful for this. Diversity is an amazing thing and both types of parents have so much to offer the sensitive child.

A NOTE FOR THE NOT-SO-SENSITIVE PARENT

You have an extraordinary capacity to use the logical part of your brain in helping your child feel calm. I am in awe of the parents I work with who can feel emotions and move through them with ease. That is not to suggest that you don't struggle with things, but when you are at your best and resourced well, I imagine you like a safely rooted tree: sturdy and grounded, wise and connected. You most likely have an ability to anchor yourself in the midst of emotional storms a little more easily than a more sensitive parent!

It can also be a challenge to understand the mind of a sensitive child when you may not experience the world in the same way. This can make these children hard to relate to at times, and understandably, you might find yourself feeling agitated or frustrated. I have worked with so many parents who feel lost as a result of this. They are incredible people and just have a 'hardier' view of the world, where things don't impact them to the same degree. They give out to themselves for wanting to roll their eyes or for feeling exasperated by their child's big feelings at times – especially when these big feelings seem to be provoked by relatively insignificant situations. Bear with me here if you are a parent who relates to this. I hope by the end of this book you will feel much more resourced and that it will feel easier to empathise with them. And please be as kind to yourselves as you can! It's not easy, and the fact you are taking the time to read this book says so much about you as a parent.

A NOTE FOR THE SENSITIVE PARENT

A sensitive parent and a sensitive child – that is certainly a lot of sensitivity in one house, as my husband often jokes. While it can be testing and challenging at the best of times, when we are well resourced this dynamic can blossom into a beautiful relationship. Your own nervous system is finely tuned and wired to react to subtleties in the environment. Your mirror neurons fire off during tantrums, meltdowns and moments of distress, meaning you have an incredible capacity for empathy. You often experience your child's pain and sadness as if it's your own. You feel it all. You have the capacity to empathise on a deep level and often understand the complex depth of processing that is happening for your child. Unfortunately, when you are not well resourced, this relationship can feel extremely difficult and lead to feelings of burnout, depletion and mental health challenges.

Think again about the window of tolerance. If you are a sensitive parent, you might notice you get bumped out of this window a little easily sometimes. This is partly due to your sensitive nervous system – naturally, parenting and other stressors are going to impact you on a deeper level. But also, due to your capacity to feel so much, your brain responds and reacts to your child's emotions as if they are happening to you too. Feeling so much emotion, thinking so reflectively and processing so much can lead to feelings of overwhelm.

A NOTE FOR BOTH

Whether we are sensitive or not so sensitive, trying to parent while managing life's other challenges, social and economic pressures and the absence of 'the village', it is completely understandable to feel overloaded sometimes. Without even diving into the more complex psychological processes at play, these factors alone can make parenting often feel exhausting.

Making sense of your past

Making sense of our own past is the biggest gift we can give our children. This is because of the finding that our child's attachment relationship to us is strongly connected to our own understanding of our early life experiences. The research shows that even if we had a difficult childhood but have been able to make sense of this experience, then we will not necessarily recreate the same patterns and can change the trajectory of our child's attachment relationship to us. This is so hopeful for any parent who worries about the impact of old patterns repeating.

I really want to reiterate how incredible our brains are – how malleable and adaptable they are and how we can *always* help ourselves and our children at any stage of our development. The reason I repeat this so frequently is I have worked with many parents who begin a shame spiral about their own parenting when they reflect on parts of themselves they find difficult that may resemble the way they were parented or that are driven from a more defensive or reactive place. Sometimes this blocks them from their own healing or from thinking too much about their own experience, as they beat themselves up for failing in some way. Please give yourself as much compassion as you can and know that we are all just doing the best we can. I would encourage you now to try and allow this chapter to be about you. We have plenty of time to think about our children and how to help them flourish, so I would love you to just focus on yourself while you read this.

If it feels safe for you to do so now, let's begin to reflect on your own childhood.

- Who was in your family when you were growing up?
- When you felt sad, worried or scared, who did you talk to?
- Who helped you when you were angry with others or with yourself?
- How did your caregivers react when you made a mistake or lied about something?
- What did your caregivers' form of discipline feel like to you when you were little?
- When you reflect on who provided you with support, warmth and nurturing, who comes to mind?
- If you have siblings, how was your relationship with them growing up?
- Do you remember if you had a playful home, and do you have memories of being played with?
- What was the general feel of your home like – for example, relaxed and calm, uptight and stressed, unpredictable and scary?
- Did you feel like you fitted in with your family – for example, did they celebrate you and your strengths, or did you receive messages that you were wrong in some way?

- Did your family experience any significant stress (financial, bereavement, trauma)?
- Did you 'fit in' as a family in your society?
- How do you think your family experiences affect your day-to-day now?
- How was school for you? Did you experience any bullying by teachers or peers?
- If you have a different learning style or needed any support (emotional or academic), was this understood and nurtured by teachers and the wider school system?
- Did you feel like you 'fitted in' with your class or with your school as a whole?

Sometimes these questions can feel upsetting to think about, so if this feels very emotive for you, it might be good to read this chapter through with someone you trust or a therapist. Reflecting on our life history can feel painful for anyone who has experienced difficulties in the past. Our family system and school system are some of our most formative experiences and have a huge influence on our developing sense of self. You might also reflect on these questions and have happy memories of your childhood, which is fantastic. Life is complex – we often have many happy memories mixed in with some more painful ones. Life is usually a wonderful messy mixture of both.

MAKING SENSE OF YOUR RESPONSES

When we begin to look more deeply into our own life history, our responses and reactions can start to make more sense. With this deeper understanding we can begin to feel more compassionate to ourselves and the way we interact in the world. Think about what it is that tends to push you out of your window of tolerance. I know we often hear this question phrased as 'What triggers you?' The word 'trigger' can feel a little harsh or make it sound like the person has control over their experience: we are triggered and then we gear up to fight! I love Bonnie Badenoch's idea of, rather than being 'triggered', thinking of it as being 'touched or awakened' by something deep down. An old wound that is raising its head. Whatever language we use to describe this experience, we can all relate to what it feels like. It can be empowering to learn more about it – especially if, like me, you tend to give yourself a hard time for your reactions and responses.

When we are growing up, we need that one person who loves us unconditionally. We need someone to comfort us when we feel sad, help us feel safe when we feel scared and remind us that we are worthy when we feel ashamed. In an ideal world, we need to know our caregivers understand us, soothe us when we are distressed and make us feel listened to and valued. This nurturing relationship sets the foundation for our emotional health into adolescence and adulthood. And in an ideal world, it is recreated again and again with teachers and significant others in our life.

Sometimes this doesn't happen in the most helpful way. This is not about blaming anyone's parents – we are all just doing our best. So many of our parents' generation and the generation before that did not have access to information about emotions and child development. They didn't know how important it is to help children feel loved, seen and understood. Without this knowledge, along with a lack of psychological support, it is understandable that some unhelpful beliefs and patterns may have repeated themselves. One of my favourite sayings is 'Well, when we look at X, Y, Z maybe it makes sense'. Maybe it makes sense that some parents did not know how to show their love or soothe an upset child, as that had never been modelled to them in their own life. So while we can hold that empathy and understanding in our minds, we may also begin to reflect on what happens for children if their emotional needs are not met.

The hard part is learning that these patterns often create a stress response in the child. When something hurtful happens to us, like feeling criticised or rejected, and we are left alone in that experience, it becomes stored in our nervous system. These little hurts are stored in our body as the physiological responses of a racing heart and tension in our face, stomach and other areas. This often happens if we haven't been seen or held in a safe, nurturing relationship with another. Being able to share our pain with someone, often through repeated storytelling and meaning making (how we make sense of our life stories), or simply being unconditionally understood by one another, helps our nervous system feel soothed. This is what co-regulation looks like. It doesn't mean that we are not still impacted by painful situations, but our body often does not encode them as traumatic when we have been truly held by another person.

We often think of trauma as the big things – the big-T traumas like heartbreaking situations of childhood abuse and neglect, war and so on. Those smaller, seemingly 'insignificant' relational pains like feeling rejected, misunderstood or ignored by important people in our life are often dismissed as 'no big deal'. The truth is, they really are a big deal. And when we are left alone to try and cope with our hurt feelings on our own, it gets stored away in our body and can be easily awakened later on. These experiences create a stress response in our body in the same way the big-T traumas do. So when something happens in the present that reminds us of a similar situation in the past, we often react and respond like it's happening all over again. An example might be feeling criticised in work by your boss, and you notice the pain and distress you experience seems to be activating a deeper hurt. This deeper hurt might be your body remembering what it felt like to be criticised by your parent when you were small. Or perhaps you feel enraged at injustice, a burning heat in your body when watching someone you love being taken advantage of. Your body remembering the excruciating pain of experiencing bullying in school by peers. The helplessness you felt when lies and rumours were spread about you becomes awakened in the present. These are just some examples of how these older relational wounds are still very much remembered by our nervous system.

We are often carrying lots of little hurts that become activated by similar situations in our everyday life. This is nobody's fault! We have to thank our limbic system and emotion centres for that. This part of our brain is the most powerful, and when we are under stress, it hijacks our thinking, rational brain and starts running the show. Unfortunately, many of us spend a lot of time in our threat system, and when this happens, we are motivated by fear and panic instead of feeling calm and connected. Our incredible brains then often try to make sense of the emotions we are experiencing by giving us a narrative, a story about why we feel anxious, sad, ashamed or scared. This narrative is often a bit skewed – it might misinterpret a situation in the present because it brings with it all of the stored pain of the past.

> *Abigail was a sensitive child who grew up with parents who gave her 'the cold shoulder' if she acted out of line. For much of her childhood she was sent alone to her room when she misbehaved to 'think about her actions', while her parents withdrew from her. They would avert their gaze from her in the morning before school, and their conversations came more out of necessity than from any real connection. Her teenage years were the hardest. Her father barely spoke to her, and she became desensitised to her mother's disappointed looks and curt responses.*
>
> *As a result of Abigail's childhood, she experiences an intense need for transparency in her communication with friends and significant others. She is hypervigilant to any hint of feeling ignored, and a lack of reply from a friend seems to awaken a deep sense of loneliness and anger that is hard for Abigail to understand. Her reactions feel so extreme to her, yet she can't seem to shift the pain and depth of her emotions. As a result of this she often falls out with friends, as they experience her as intense and feel like she holds them to very high standards. They try to explain that they didn't not reply on purpose, but Abigail is suspicious of this and can't help feeling rejected.*

This is a common example of how older relational wounds are remembered by our nervous system and may impact our relationships in the present. If you are reading this and some of it sounds familiar, please know that we have enormous potential to help ourselves with this. Sometimes it is enough to talk these things through with someone who you know really loves you and whom you have a connected relationship with. And sometimes, if there is a lot of pain there, this healing might happen in the context of a safe therapeutic relationship, where a therapist helps you to touch on these more painful parts of you with compassionate, non-judgemental and soothing care. A non-judgemental, soothing, connected relationship is, in an ideal world, what we all need to feel in our most calm and regulated state and helps us heal from painful experiences in the past.

If you take one thing away from this chapter, I would love it to be that we are social creatures and that healing and regulation happen in the context of safe relationships. In order to really be in close, connected relationships with others, we have to work on coming out of our threat system and allowing ourselves to be vulnerable.

THE SIGNIFICANCE OF OUR INNER DIALOGUE

One of the things that can make us feel disconnected from ourselves and others is our own inner dialogue. Our 'inner critic' and our 'inner worrier' often develop from our early life experiences. Times when we felt embarrassed, shamed, scared all are stored in our nervous system. This system holds on tightly to these experiences as a way of protecting us from being hurt again in the future. I spoke earlier about 'neuroception' – that our brains are always scanning for threat and safety, as it is so important for our survival. These memories and experiences are stored to help guide us away from what is safe or unsafe. Unfortunately, sometimes this threat detector has been finely tuned from lots of hurtful experiences in the past, and thus many of us have a strong internal protector that doesn't always feel like it is helping us!

You might know what it feels like to be your own biggest critic. This critical voice often so closely resembles our own that we don't realise how harsh it can be and the impact it might be having on us. Think about how you talk to yourself. Are you generally quite understanding and kind to yourself? Or do you tend to hold yourself to high standards and then beat yourself up if you fall short in some way? Or maybe you keep others at a distance because you hear 'What's the point – people just let you down', and not needing to rely on others feels like the safest option. Perhaps you are always comparing yourself to others or beating yourself up for being 'too weak', 'too soft' or 'not a good enough person or parent', believing deep down that you are flawed in some way.

I have worked with many incredible clients who say things like: 'I shouldn't need anyone else, Aoife. I should be able to manage on my own. I feel so weak for finding things hard – others get on just fine by themselves.' Our culture really values individualism, and we have come to believe that being strong means we should be able to cope with life's challenges alone, that needing others somehow makes us less than. I wish more people understood that our whole survival and existence depends on our connection and relationship with others.

We see this too with the dangers of comparative suffering. This is when we compare our experience to another's and believe we should be better able to manage things, as the other person is struggling more than us. Of course being able to shift our perspective and have awareness of and empathy for others who are going through painful circumstances is really important. But just because your experiences are not as challenging as someone else's, it doesn't mean that it is not impacting you and that you don't deserve help. Many of my clients say things like: 'I feel stupid being here. I am taking a space from someone else who really needs it. I am wasting your time.' While our life circumstances all differ, and we always want to be mindful of the painful situations others are in, there is no hierarchy when it comes to psychological pain. And usually when we scratch the surface, these clients are going through huge amounts of stress and overwhelm. So for any parent reading this who feels like a failure or who beats themselves up for not being able to just 'suck it up' and cope better, please remember that if it was that easy, we would all do it! Our brains and nervous systems are so much more complex than that.

> *Sam is a father of a four-year-old little girl called Maria. She is a sensitive child who has always shown a strong preference for being around her mom, Mary. This makes sense, as Mary is her primary caregiver and works inside the home, so they spend the most time together. Sam tries*

his best to connect with Maria but is becoming more and more disheartened by her only wanting her mom and what feels like her consistent rejection of him. Mary is exhausted from being the one who is needed all of the time and has little energy left to give to her relationship with Sam. Feeling disconnected from both Maria and Mary begins to take a toll on Sam. He feels lonely and angry with himself for his emotions. This manifests as agitation at home and snapping more frequently at both of them. The painful part of this cycle is that Maria is extremely attuned to her parents' emotions. So when she senses this agitation and frustration towards her, she is even less likely to want to spend time with Sam. This pattern starts a difficult feedback loop that keeps Sam on the outside and leaves Maria feeling confused and sad about her relationship with him.

Sam's thoughts begin to consist of critical thoughts that sound like: 'Grow up, Sam! You feel rejected by a four-year-old – you're pathetic'. 'No wonder Mary doesn't want to be around you; she doesn't even look at you anymore. Stop feeling so sorry for yourself.' 'You're always in bad form – who could blame them for not wanting to be around you!'

These thoughts are further amplified by the fact that Sam grew up believing that vulnerability is a weakness. He grew up in a culture that valued men for being 'strong' and a patriarchal society that heavily influenced the idea that 'being a man' meant he should not feel vulnerable. Due to his own experiences during childhood, he has been conditioned to believe that true strength comes from powering on through and distracting from painful feelings. He has learned how to wear his protective suit of armour and to push down his feelings. This pattern of coping often works well, protecting him from feelings like sadness and loneliness that bubble away under the surface, protecting him from the quiet whispers that he is not good enough or strong enough because he is human enough to feel. While his suit of armour helps him feel safe, it also unfortunately keeps him feeling disconnected and lonely. This is because it activates his 'fight' response, and his predominant emotion is anger.

Sam's already-stressed nervous system gets tipped further out of his window of tolerance and into hyperarousal, and his anger is mostly directed towards himself and a short fuse with his family. If we know that deep down Sam needs to feel like he matters, to feel seen and loved, but his behaviour is that of pushing others away, then it makes sense that his painful emotions continue to go unmet. It also makes sense that as a way of coping with this he continues to put on a suit of armour and pushes any vulnerability as far out of his conscious mind as he can.

Ideally, we can all begin to slow down enough to tune in and recognise the impact our thoughts are having on us. Tuning into our own vulnerability is so helpful because it is from this place that we can access what we need. We might work on saying to our critic, 'Hey, I hear you. I know you think you're trying to help, but constantly beating me up like this is making me feel sad and ashamed. I need you to give me a bit of space and recognise I am doing my best.' In an ideal world, we have someone who sees our vulnerability and pain and meets us there with kindness, love and compassion.

Sam is so used to wearing his suit of armour that he finds it hard to access his emotions. His sadness is difficult for him to understand, and his anger feels safer, as it is so familiar. This protective pattern of coping is blocking him from being able to connect with his wife, leading him to feel alone and disconnected. If you recognise this happening in your relationships, it might be helpful to begin practising saying how you feel. This might feel uncomfortable at first, but the research shows that the more we practise allowing ourselves to be vulnerable, the easier it becomes and the more connected we feel in our relationships. Below is a conversation Sam has with his wife.

> *Sam: I know I have been stressed lately, and I just wanted to say how sorry I am for being in bad form all the time. I'm not entirely sure what's wrong, but if I'm being honest, I think I feel a bit lonely, Mary. I am finding it so hard to cope with Maria – I feel like she doesn't like me – and I feel like we never have time together anymore either. I always wanted to be a fun, kind dad and a loving partner, but I feel like I have failed at that. I have been so angry lately because I just feel so angry with myself. I know that sounds pathetic, and I'm embarrassed saying this out loud.*

Mary: I'm so sorry you have been feeling this way, Sam. I have been finding the way you are behaving at home hard, as it feels like we're walking on eggshells sometimes around you, but that makes a lot of sense. I really miss spending time with you too. We love you no matter what, and you have not failed us! Let's work on having you more involved with Maria – I know it will change in time, Sam, so try not to worry too much. Let's keep talking about it, though, as much as we can, and thank you for being so honest.

Sam: I wish I had been more open with you sooner. Thank you so much for understanding. I will work on this, and I don't want there to be a distance between us anymore. I have really missed you and I love you and Maria so much.

There is huge power in vulnerability. What we see here is Mary and Sam being open and honest with each other, which allows them to connect again. When we speak from the parts of ourselves that feel sad, ashamed, scared or lonely, it is a lot easier for the other person to really hear us. When we speak from our coping protectors and our defences, unfortunately our loved ones often speak from theirs too. Our 'protectors and defences' are our brain's incredibly powerful coping strategy that evolves to do exactly as the name describes: to protect or defend us from experiencing painful emotions and feeling too vulnerable. While these psychological protectors make sense, often giving us a sense of safety, control and predictability, they also make it much more difficult to resolve any difficulties because one or both people are detached from their pain. When we slow down and tune into ourselves long enough to listen to what's going on, it is much easier to see what we really need. Those needs are usually to feel seen and understood. To feel loved and cared for. To feel safe in our relationships and reminded that we matter.

I know in reality it is hard to be vulnerable and to openly talk about how we feel. However, it is a huge myth in our society that vulnerability is a weakness. Vulnerability is a massive strength: it takes great amounts of courage and bravery to be honest. It is hard to do this when we fear being judged by others. The problem is when we push down our emotions and pretend we are okay it takes a toll on our emotional and physical health. We feel burnt out, drained, irritable, anxious, depressed. It is also isolating because we really believe we are the only ones feeling this way. Remember, the antidote to shame is empathy and connection. The more we talk about these things and normalise finding things hard, the more understood and seen we feel and therefore the less ashamed. In the words of Dr Brené Brown, 'Vulnerability is not weakness, it's our greatest measure of courage.'

Compassionate guides

Becoming more aware of the judgemental thoughts we all have towards ourselves sometimes (like we are not good enough parents or failing in some way) can be a huge step in beginning to be more compassionate to ourselves as parents. Recognising that our responses and reactions are an understandable response to our environment, to our internal struggles, can help us take action. I would encourage you to talk to other people about how you are feeling. I believe that the story we are telling ourselves can change when we feel supported and understood. I love this quote from Ann Voskamp: 'Shame dies when stories are told in safe places.' So whether it is a friend, partner or therapist, please don't suffer alone.

Another idea that might help you to feel more compassionate to yourself is to become aware of your body language and facial expressions. Practise noticing what your physiological state is when you feel stressed or anxious, how it manifests in your body when your thoughts become particularly loud. Maybe you notice you bite your nails, pick your skin, clench your jaw, tighten your muscles or furrow your brows. This is often an indication we are feeling overwhelmed, and our nervous system is doing its best to regulate. Awareness of this is the most important step. If we notice we are doing this, we might then stand up, if possible. We might work on relaxing our muscles, take a few deep breaths.

We have more nerve endings in our face than anywhere else in our body. Neuroscience research shows us that, not only do we show how we feel on our face, but our face also tells us *what* to feel. This is fascinating if, like me, you often have a worried look or a furrowed brow. The powerful receptors in our brain interpret this as stress and anxiety, so relaxing our face and jaw is a quick and effective way of helping our nervous system feel calm. We can take this a step further by bringing our mouth into a half-smiling position. This helps release serotonin (a chemical in our brain that plays a key role in our mood), which makes us feel more regulated and calmer.

Most of all, we want to practise being gently curious about

our life and the way we act in the world. We want to become highly aware of the way we talk to ourselves, the tone of voice and the language we use. If you can, write down a few points in your journal about your self-critic or your inner worrier. How do you know when it's been awakened? What does it sound like? Does it remind you of anyone from your past? Or maybe it's just a general sense – it could be a shape or a colour. Get to know it and begin to examine it with compassion and curiosity. Our goal is not to get rid of it completely, but to help it soften its grip on us and notice the impact it's having. To build up that compassionate side of us that can stand back and say, 'Hey! Hey, what's going on here?' – the way you would to someone you love in your life and wanted to protect. Imagine being your own best friend and speaking to yourself the way you would to them. It takes a lot of practice to relax the grip these thoughts have on us, but I promise it's worth it!

WE ARE RELATIONAL BEINGS

Your challenges and struggles are not just an intrinsic problem. Unfortunately, as a society, we tend to believe we should be able to cope with challenges alone, and we forget that self-regulation happens best in co-regulation. We are relational beings, so in an ideal world, our challenges and struggles should not be seen as something we need to deal with on our own. Healing happens in the context of connected relationships – in having another person that we can talk to and share our worries and concerns with: a friend, a partner, a therapist, someone we can feel safe with and who listens with gentleness and care.

RAIN OF SELF-COMPASSION

If you in any way relate to Sam and are someone for whom anxiety and critical thoughts feel like just another part of who you are, here's a guide that might help you. This is a self-compassion exercise adapted from one of Tara Brach's wonderful meditations. It is called the RAIN of self-compassion and is one of the most powerful practices we can implement. It simply means: *recognise* what is going on, *allow* the experience to be there, *investigate* with interest and care, and *nurture* with self-compassion.

Find a comfortable position, away from any distractions or noise (that might be asking a lot, I know!), for a few moments while we think through this as intentionally as possible together.

Recognise what is going on – start by observing your thoughts with gentle curiosity. Don't try to push them away or challenge them: just slow down and take the time to really listen to them.

Let your intention go inward and focus on your breath, breathing in long and deep, filling your chest and your lungs. Now, focusing on a slow out-breath, feel the sensation as your breath leaves your body. Again, focus on a deep in-breath, and then a slow out-breath with a sense of letting go. And one more time, inhaling deeply and a slow out-breath, just letting go. Allow your breath to come back into a natural, soothing rhythm.

Take a moment to scan through your body and become aware of any areas of tightness. Feel your face, noticing any tension across your forehead, eyes and jaw. Just allow everything to soften if you can. Notice what your shoulders feel like and release any stress that you might be holding. Open your chest as you take the next in-breath and soften your tummy as you exhale. Focus as best you can on soothing breathing and widen your awareness to your whole body and any tension you might be holding.

Scan inward and notice any feelings that are there. Maybe it's a feeling of helplessness, depletion, sadness or anger. Now bring your awareness to your inner critical voice and notice what it sounds like. You might be being particularly hard on yourself for how you're feeling, judging yourself for your behaviours, for your parenting or for who you are as a person.

Pause and recognise what's happening. Notice what's most predominant. It might be that inner critical voice or a feeling of fear, anxiety, shame, agitation or distress. It can help here to just name it: 'Ah, self-judgement, self-aversion, anger, fear.'

Allow the experience to be there – this means that we just let whatever we are feeling be there. Acknowledge the reality without pushing it away. This might sound like: 'Oh, wow. There you are, inner critic. Hello. You are quite loud today.'

Investigate with interest and care – begin an investigation within your body, noticing what sensations you are experiencing with curiosity and gentleness. How is this feeling showing up inside me? Where do I notice it? Do you feel it in your throat, in your chest or your tummy?

Nurture with self-compassion – wherever you feel anything a little more strongly, it can be helpful to just put your hand there. This can deepen your awareness of where the pain is. You're inviting whatever is there to come forward. You might ask yourself, 'What's the worst part of this?' And breathe with what's there. Tune into this part of you and ask yourself, 'What does this part of me most need? How does it want me to be with it?' See if you can offer some message of care. You might put your hand on your heart or give yourself a hug.

Or you might just send yourself the message 'You're okay', or 'It's understandable you feel so deeply sad right now', 'It's okay to feel the way you do – it's so painful knowing so many people are suffering' and offer self-compassion. And if it's really hard for you to do that, think of the kindness and warmth that flows through someone you trust. Or if that's also hard, maybe it's an animal or a spiritual figure that guides you. Just imagine that care flowing into you, into the vulnerable place and the pain you're holding on to. It might help to imagine a big wave of light flowing into you, minding you as it wraps warmth around you. When you're ready, return your attention to your breath, and after a few deep breaths, ground yourself again in the room.

I know an exercise like this can be so hard to do, so well done for giving it a try. It really does get easier the more we practise. Be kind to yourselves for any judgements that show up around this and know that it is so human to struggle with tuning into our emotions in this way, particularly during challenging times.

CHAPTER 4

How we learn to protect ourselves

Understanding why we feel certain emotions strongly or why we struggle with certain behaviours in ourselves and our children is very helpful for us in our parenting journey. The more awareness we have about our patterns – how we tend to cope with stress – the more we can consciously respond to both ourselves and our children. This helps us become more attuned to ourselves and more connected to each other. I am a huge advocate for speaking about these different 'parts' we all have, without blame, judgement or shame.

What is a 'protector'?

When we experience painful situations in our life, we often experience a split from our genuine, authentic self, and wounded related parts of us manifest as coping 'protectors' to help us to manage overwhelming experiences. It is important for healing that we understand that these parts of us are trying to protect us and keep us safe.

We often dislike these different parts of us, our 'protectors', and we feel ashamed or judge ourselves for having these pieces of our personality that become activated under stress. I hope that this chapter will help you to see that we have so much to thank these parts for, and there is always a function in the ways we have learned to cope. Most of all, I hope you always remember we are all human. And being human means we all have wounds, we all have a story, and we are always growing and evolving.

If we think back to neuroception (how our brains are constantly scanning for cues of threat and cues of safety), you might remember how all children need to feel secure, loved and understood to develop a sense of safety in the world and with their caregivers. When this happens, it creates a buffer around our brain and nervous system that makes us more resilient to the inevitable stressors life will throw our way.

Conversely, growing up in a house where you don't feel understood, connected to, valued or safe can lead to attachment wounds that can change how your brain develops. Being in a school environment that is not helpful, experiencing bullying, being from a marginalised population or being misunderstood over time can cause significant stress in our nervous system. It can affect our immune system, our hormonal system and our DNA. This is because our stress-response system is activated again and again if we feel ignored, shamed or scared or when we don't feel valued and understood. When this happens, children engage in powerful psychological survival strategies that help them cope with the situation. These psychological 'protectors', as Bonnie Badenoch calls them, were extremely helpful at the time, but unfortunately they do not always serve us well as we move on in life.

You might wonder why emotional closeness can feel scary sometimes, why you find it hard to be your true self. Or maybe you wonder why you are so hard on yourself or why you are stuck repeating the same patterns even when you know they are unhelpful. Or perhaps there is a part of you that often feels hopeless, that, when activated, spirals downwards into preventing you from moving forward and twists your thinking into 'what's the point'. Or a part that feels injustice towards the world and, when activated, feels angry and let down. You might recognise this when you feel like 'no one cares' or 'everyone is selfish'. Although these can be difficult parts to sit with, they are usually trying so hard to advocate for us and need us to pay attention to the pain that is underneath. This often involves tuning in and recognising they are hurt because their upset has not been acknowledged and understood. It usually means that an earlier injustice has happened that is needing to be heard. Or perhaps there's a part of you that feels anxious, always needing to be on guard. Or a depressed part that wants to hide away. Or a sceptical part that has learned not to trust people easily, to be wary of other intentions. But something to keep in mind while thinking about these parts is 'What is this part of me trying to say?' We want to practise listening to them with gentle curiosity, rather than pushing them away. If you struggle with these different parts, a book called *No Bad Parts* by Dr Richard C. Schwartz may be a help, along with working with a therapist to guide you. When someone who cares about us wants to listen to all of the parts of us, advocating for them and their feelings, it helps us become an advocate for ourselves.

PEOPLE-PLEASING AS A PSYCHOLOGICAL PROTECTOR

A few months ago, I was packing late at night for a flight we had two days later. I was already frustrated with myself for doing everything so last-minute as usual. My son was jumping around with excitement, taking all the clothes back out of the case. My husband was also exhausted, both of our nervous systems on edge from a few weeks of heightened sensitivity and behaviour that had been difficult to manage. Neither of us had had much sleep, as we have two little koalas who wake frequently throughout the night. My husband asked me for my passport to check in for the flight. I watched as a look of concern and disappointment crossed his face, and he told me my passport was out of date. I immediately felt my stomach sink, and thoughts loudly rushed into my head – 'You're so stupid, Aoife! How are you so unorganised? You've just ruined the holiday for everyone' – and I felt that familiar feeling of shame.

My son, still unaware anything was wrong, continued to jump around in delight. 'Stop!' I shouted, angrily raising my voice while pulling the suitcase out of his reach. I turned my back and heard nothing but silence for a minute or two. When I turned back around, I saw a crumpled-up little face as he released a deep, painful cry, no longer able to hold in the tears. His big eyes looked up at me in fear and confusion.

This story might resonate with you on some level. We are all perfectly imperfect humans and will all raise our voices or act in unhelpful ways sometimes when we are overwhelmed. And while it is important and helpful to bring awareness to our behaviours so that we can work on them, try not to be too hard on yourself. In these moments, remind yourself how challenging life can be and how understandable it is to feel stressed, especially when we have been pushed out of our window of tolerance. We will talk more about our children in these situations and how we can help them, but for now, let's stay with what happened for me as a parent.

I was flooded with guilt and shame. The logical part of my brain and nervous system knew this would be fine and he would be okay once I regulated myself, apologised and helped him feel safe by connecting with him. However, the emotional part of my brain was transported back in time, and I felt rooted to the spot, frozen in some childlike state that felt scared and confused. I suddenly saw myself reflected in his eyes and somehow knew exactly how he felt – how confusing it feels to be excited one moment and scared the next.

Two things happened then. The first was that seeing his upset and distress activated my own mirror neuron system, meaning I could feel his sadness and fear on a physiological level. This is a common experience if you are an empathic person – we often feel other people's pain and sadness as if it is our own. The second thing was that my own inner-child wounding was touched on and activated by my son's response. It was the latter that activated not just my empathy but also my more complex protector known as 'people-pleasing'. I became consumed with checking he was okay and felt so anxious that I had caused a rupture in our relationship. I found myself asking him 'Are you my friend? I'm sorry' the same way a child might do with a parent. The logical part of my brain recognised this behaviour was strange – my son appeared to be okay once I gave him a big hug and said I was sorry. Despite this, my activated coping protector was stuck in the zone of hyperarousal, and I became consumed with making sure he was happy with me. This translated into difficulty holding boundaries with him and trying everything possible to make up for my actions. This wasn't stemming from a grounded and connected repair with my child, as I was stuck in a fawn response.

You might recognise this behaviour with your children or in your other relationships: a compulsive need to make sure everything is okay and a deep sense of unease if someone is angry with you or if you feel like you have done something wrong. When this becomes activated, we have become disconnected from ourselves, and our anxiety is fuelling our thoughts and behaviour. Becoming aware of how this shows up in our life is the first step in helping ourselves with it. In my work with parents, I often see this pattern of coping become activated when a child has a big reaction to a boundary that the parent has set. Sometimes our child's upset, or anger can evoke wounds we are carrying in our heart. From this place we may find it hard to hold a boundary because feeling like we have hurt someone we love feels so uncomfortable.

For example, let's say the sensitive child cries and doesn't want to leave the playground. Their parent is exhausted, running on empty and hasn't eaten since breakfast. They feel anxious that their child will be angry with them, so they respond with 'Okay, we will stay longer'. In these moments their own needs don't matter anymore – *they* don't matter. This parent may find it difficult to say no and to hold boundaries because their self-worth is associated with making sure they don't offend others. This pattern of people-pleasing continues to play out with their children, as the parent fears feeling rejected by them. The challenge here is that this parent is becoming disconnected from themselves, and it may build resentment and frustration towards their child and in their other relationships. Unfortunately, it also can lead to challenges for our children, as gentle boundaries and limits help them feel safe. This parent might need support in learning how to hold space for their child's emotions without feeling like they are responsible for their upset. They may benefit from learning how to hold compassionate and gentle boundaries and how to soothe their own stress system when they feel scared, guilty or like they have done something wrong. And most of all, learning how to be kinder to themselves and remembering it's important to take care of themselves too. They might do this by empathising with their child: 'I am sorry, love – I know it's hard to leave the playground. I get it. And we need to go home.' Boundaries can be kind and understanding, while also being clear and firm. We need to take a deep breath ourselves through our children's big feelings, knowing that their feelings make so much sense and so do ours. It is more than okay to say no! Our children pick up on this over time. They see we get it, and our empathy towards their frustration helps them more than we realise. They also come to learn and accept our compassionate, clear and firm boundaries.

Let's have a deeper look at people-pleasing as a coping protector. This is a complex and powerful survival strategy often learned in childhood as a way of protecting us from psychological pain. For example, we often observe this in children who are frequently criticised and who fear disappointing their parents. They learn quickly that pleasing others will protect them from the pain of not feeling good enough. We also often see its origins in school, when being part of 'the tribe' is so important. Feeling left out or excluded is particularly painful when we are growing up, and children often learn how to fit in by pushing down their own needs so they will be accepted in their peer group. This protector is helpful at the time, but unfortunately it often leads to us feeling lonely inside, anxious and disconnected, as we are not showing our true selves. Our needs to feel seen, accepted and loved for who we are continue to go unmet.

Many sensitive people are labelled as people-pleasers, and their behaviour is often understood through this lens. This is complicated because sensitive people are naturally very empathic – they feel other people's emotions on a deep level and thus are naturally driven to help them. They often have an intuitive sense about other people's pain and sometimes might be less assertive about their own needs if they don't want to hurt others. Their big hearts might be what other people value in them, and it can be harder for them to hold boundaries or push back in certain situations. I don't think it is an either/or way of being in the world. I think that being empathic and being a people-pleaser are at times closely connected, but whatever lens we view this through, the cost of caring 'too much', people-pleasing or putting others' needs above our own is unfortunately high.

If this sounds familiar to you, know that it is possible to be a person who cares deeply but who recognises when you are putting other people's feelings before your own. One small step is to become aware of the way this can show up in your life or in your relationships. This might be as simple as saying, 'Ah, hey there. I hear you. I know you are the part of me that feels uneasy sometimes and wants to keep everyone happy. I see you and I am listening. Thank you for trying to help me, but I wonder if I'm being authentic to myself in this?' You might then pay attention to when you don't stick up for yourself because you are aware of hurting someone else. Practise slowing down and tuning into your own feelings, acknowledging this part of you while also recognising it may not always be helpful. It might feel uncomfortable at first to say no, to hold boundaries with your child, to have difficult conversations, to ask for what you need, to highlight the behaviours of others in your life that are not helpful, to question your relationships with people who don't appreciate you, to take more time for yourself, to prioritise things that are important for your mental health. But the more you do this, even by one small step every day, it wires those connections in your brain that remind you how much you matter too.

PERFECTIONISM AS A PSYCHOLOGICAL PROTECTOR

We have all heard the term 'perfectionism' and you might relate to it as a parent or in work, sport or relationships. So many of us put pressure on ourselves to be the perfect parent, to do everything right, to know it all. And a lot of the time we are measuring our self-worth by impossibly high standards. Perfectionism is another psychological survival strategy that is often learned during childhood as a way of keeping us safe and to help protect us from experiencing painful emotions, like feeling ashamed. It often develops in response to being criticised or if a lot of emphasis was placed on our achievements and not as much on emotional connection. If you also happen to be a sensitive person, criticism can feel especially painful because your brain is wired to feel things deeply. We might believe 'If I do everything right then I won't open myself up to criticism and I never have to feel like I'm not good enough'.

Although this is incredibly adaptive, it unfortunately causes problems as time goes on. It creates a lot of stress, anxiety and pressure. Negative feedback or any perceived criticism is felt deep in your bones, and time feels like it freezes over. Anyone who experiences perfectionism knows the sense of angst and unease that is intertwined with it. When things are going well, we feel great, and our brain produces endorphins from the validation we receive from others. Sadly, this is often short-lived as, inevitably, we can't do everything 'right' all the time. So when something happens and we don't live up to the standards we expect, we feel angry towards ourselves and deeply ashamed. This can push us out of our window of tolerance, and we might begin to feel very anxious or low and flat. We might feel so stressed about the task at hand that we procrastinate, stuck in our freeze response, and begin to feel immobilised.

The parent being driven by perfectionism may never ask for help because that would be confirmation that they are not coping. They often have an inner critic so strong that anxious racing thoughts are considered normal. They experience constant pressure to 'try harder, be better'. They live frequently in their sympathetic nervous system and may feel extremely anxious when their child acts in ways that they perceive have let them down. Their six-year-old screaming in a supermarket? Their nine-year-old being rude to their friend? They may feel that this is confirmation they are not a good enough parent, and this anger can't help being directed towards their child. Perfectionism also often leads us to compare. We might compare our parenting or how our children are behaving and see this as a reflection of our self-worth, which leads us to feel anxious in ourselves and frustrated and angry with our children. This can be particularly challenging if we have a sensitive child who is more vocal, more intense and reactive to their environment. These children are wonderful, but their behaviour can be more challenging to understand as they are feeling everything so much.

If we are driven by perfectionism, it is easy to forget that many factors influence a child's development, behaviours and responses. Parenting can feel so stressful for the perfectionist parent who might internalise these as a reflection of who they are. This can be heightened around family or other people whom you feel judged by.

> *I was in a social setting recently with a group of people I don't know very well. Being someone who is highly aware of others' moods and behaviours, I watched these people closely as they interpreted the behaviour of one of my children. My son was feeling overwhelmed at being in a new setting with lots of people. He hadn't eaten much that morning, as he was stressed that he was being rushed somewhere, and most likely was feeling anxious. So, hunger, anxiety and the sensory overstimulation of lots of noise and a busy environment resulted in a meltdown. One of the well-intentioned parents said to me, 'Oh, wow! Mine used to do this – you need to nip this in the bud quick! He needs to know that is absolutely not okay.'*
>
> *I was surprised at how I acted in this scenario. I am lucky to have a lot of knowledge about brain development, and I knew this behaviour was not intentional, but rather an overwhelmed little nervous system that needed connection. Even with this knowledge, I felt embarrassed because I thought I was being judged. In that moment I felt irritated with my son, I was tipped out of my window, and my perfectionist protector was activated. Rather than taking the time to co-regulate with my son, which is all he really*

needed, I felt anxious and pleaded with him to stop. My thoughts sounded like: 'They are all judging me. This is so embarrassing – stop letting me down.' My behaviour towards him was much less gentle than usual. And without the usual response from me of connection and validation, you can imagine how the rest of the story plays out. Everything escalated further, with my son confused about his behaviour and feeling unsafe in his relationship with me. I left shortly afterwards and was so upset with myself the whole way home.

If this is something that happens to you too, I hope you practise being really kind to yourself. So many of us have grown up in a culture where our behaviour was often responded to with a strict approach that valued being polite and socially acceptable more than tuning into the needs of the child. As a result of this, sometimes these deeply ingrained thoughts become awakened in us. You might notice these thoughts become particularly loud when you are with family or other people in your life that you feel judged by. This is really common, and I have worked with many parents who find this challenging. If we remember that the onset of these complex psychological protectors usually begins in childhood, then it makes sense that they might be awakened when we are in similar environments. Awareness of this is huge, and having a little mantra that you can practise saying to yourself is a big help. 'Oh, I hear you, perfectionist part. I know you worry we are being judged. I see you trying to get everything right, and I know you are feeling anxious. This is so hard, I know – let's take a deep breath and try and tune into our wise self.' And practise tuning into this with as much compassion as you can. You can acknowledge this part of you while also stepping back into your wise self, who reminds you that you are only human and that you are doing the best you can.

Something else that has helped me dramatically with this is a deep knowing that our children's big emotions are a natural and expected part of their development. I really believe if we can grasp this on a visceral level, we no longer feel ashamed or embarrassed about behaviour. We begin to take a curious and gentle approach to figuring out what is beneath it, knowing that it is often the most challenging behaviour that has the most upset or hurt underneath. If we practise leaning into this with connection and care, the behaviour often melts away. This helps our children to feel safe with us and know that they can rely on us to meet their needs. Of course we won't be able to do that all of the time, and it's normal to feel frustrated sometimes – parenting is so hard! But for the most part, this heightened awareness will help us feel more confident and grounded as parents.

SELF-SOOTHING AS A PSYCHOLOGICAL PROTECTOR

Another psychological survival strategy is our self-soothing protector. This is complicated because self-soothing is a fantastic way of helping us to feel more regulated and at ease. We could all probably do with being a little better at soothing ourselves when we are sad, anxious or experiencing other painful emotions. When we are soothing ourselves in healthy ways, we are still feeling the pain but making it easier to move through by being kind to ourselves. Examples might include taking a warm bath, ringing a friend, getting outside in nature. I have included some more ideas for grounding and soothing ourselves at the end of this chapter, but for now, let's focus on what a self-soothing protector looks like. This psychological survival strategy often begins in childhood. Soothing through detaching from painful emotions is a powerful way of regulating a stressed nervous system. It helps numb and soothe hurt feelings, anxiety, sadness, shame and loneliness. A child may begin to comfort eat or excessively use video games and so on as a way of escaping psychological pain. These distraction techniques often provide temporary relief to a nervous system in distress. While this makes so much sense, unfortunately we don't learn how to tune into the pain we are experiencing by allowing ourselves to feel and express it – we learn how to numb or escape these feelings instead. Over time, this can lead us towards addiction, eating difficulties and other forms of understandable but challenging behaviours.

Let's have a look at Liam's story to help us make sense of this.

When Liam was growing up, he always felt a little bit different. He was the youngest of two boys and grew up in a family that valued achievements in sports and academics. His father found it particularly challenging that Liam wasn't anywhere near top of his class in either. His brother was gifted at football and seemed to breeze through academics. Liam was highly attuned to his father's comments and disappointment from a young age. He describes his mother as a kind person, but she would often refer to him as lazy and compared him to his brother. He wanted his father to be proud of him, so he pushed himself as hard as he could in sports and school. Despite his best efforts, he was not picked for the school teams and his test results always fell within the average range. From a very young age Liam felt ashamed. If we remember that the only way children can make sense of their world is to turn inward, it makes sense that he interpreted this as 'I am unlovable; I will never be good enough'. He didn't want to open up to his mother too much either, as he felt she would think he was overthinking things, that he was too sensitive and a bit 'over the top'.

Liam had many friends but always kept people at a distance. The psychological protector he developed to keep himself from experiencing painful emotions like shame was to detach and avoid his feelings. He immersed himself in video games and spent long periods of time alone in his room. He would sleep, read or play his video games for hours on end as a way of tuning out the pain underneath. This repeated pattern of distraction and soothing began to wire into his nervous system. When Liam was first introduced to alcohol, it was the first time in his life that he felt really at ease – stress seemed to just melt away and he experienced a new feeling he had never had before: confidence and calm. His alcohol intake was always higher than his friends', but he normalised this to himself by having a busy social life. He continued to distract and soothe his nervous system through work, exercise and binge-watching television.

Liam is in a loving relationship with his partner Kevin for eight years. He describes their relationship as 'good' but does not open up to Kevin about his emotions. Kevin describes Liam as a kind, caring and fun person but also describes him as quite aloof. Being an introvert, Kevin was initially drawn to Liam's active social life and admired his outgoing nature. As the years have gone on, Kevin has noticed Liam has a pattern of avoiding emotions and he is starting to feel disconnected from him.

They adopted a little girl called Lucy six years ago. Everything was fine for the first few years of Lucy's life. She was, for the most part, quite easy to manage, and they had a close and connected relationship. At the age of five, Lucy was bullied by two girls in her class. She would come home from school upset and look for connection and reassurance. Liam noticed he felt agitated by Lucy's behaviour. He had little tolerance for this reassurance-seeking and wanted her to just be able to move on. He found her repeated looping about these two girls highly irritating and wished she would stop. He also noticed his urge to numb his own emotions through work and alcohol increased.

Our children trigger our unmet needs from when we were little. It's the inner child in Liam that is being activated by Lucy's upset. When Liam was small, his emotions were experienced as 'too much' by his parents. They were agitated by them, and he was seen as too sensitive. So now when Lucy expresses her painful emotions, he feels triggered by this. He has never learned how to soothe his own emotions in a helpful way and be kind to himself, so it is understandable that he feels frustrated by Lucy. He is also feeling ashamed about his numbing and soothing strategies. He knows he is stuck in this cycle but feels so overwhelmed that alcohol is providing his anxious brain with a much-needed break. Liam needs help here to begin some innerchild healing work that will allow him to tune into his vulnerable feelings and slowly learn how to soothe himself in more helpful ways. He needs support and kindness to feel safe enough to peel back the layers and learn how to treat himself with compassion so that he can begin to treat Lucy with that same understanding and care.

I wish more people understood that this self-soothing pattern is an understandable response to an overwhelmed nervous system. The first step here, again, is awareness. We can begin to shine a spotlight on behaviour we might be engaging in as a way of soothing a stressed system, being a curious and kind voice that wonders if these habits are aligned with our values. It's not necessarily that we need to completely abstain (although that can be the best option sometimes) from habits that might not be the most helpful. We are human and all just doing our best! But if we recognise these patterns are occurring as a way of numbing pain, then actively trying another form of soothing our stress system will be very helpful over time. This softens our self-soothing numbing pattern and creates new neural pathways in our brain that help us feel more connected to ourselves and to others. The more we do this, our brain and nervous system learn 'Oh, cool, there are other ways I can soothe here'.

An example might be going out for a walk or a run rather than having an alcoholic drink to unwind. Maybe it looks like intentionally moving away from the laptop in the evening and reading a book instead. Perhaps it is being mindful of our scrolling habits on our phone and doing something creative we enjoy, like drawing or painting. It often looks like calling a friend or having a conversation with someone we love rather than binge-watching television on our own. The difficulty with all of this is that often people feel so ashamed of their habits that they do not look for support. They try and combat it alone and it is incredibly difficult for any of us to do that. If we think back to Liam, we can understand how shame may get in the way of Liam asking for help. He experiences critical thoughts about how much easier life seems to be for those around him and how weak he is by comparison. He is furious with himself for his cravings, and exhausted managing the irritability and agitation that goes along with them. The cycle often leads him to increase his alcohol consumption rather than decrease it. If you are a parent who relates to Liam in this way, please don't struggle alone. Your behaviours and patterns of soothing do not define who you are. Remind yourself that when we are stressed our nervous system craves to feel at ease and calm. Some of us have a wiring that actively seeks out more dopamine (our brain's feel-good hormone) to feel a sense of soothing or for a lift in mood. There are many reasons this is the case – our stress and overwhelm plays a role, as does our genetics. Our dopamine receptors are influenced by our patterns of soothing in the past, any history of using substances and mental health difficulties we may have experienced. I quit smoking many years ago, yet during particularly stressful periods, my brain still reminds me, 'Oh! You're stressed, Aoife. Nicotine is something that helped you in the past.' It is fascinating how powerful our reward-seeking centres are under stress.

The quick effects of the more unhelpful patterns of soothing often come as a welcome relief to a nervous system that is in a hypervigilant state. This is not your fault and is always something that we can rewire and help ourselves with. Remember that empathy is the antidote to shame, and that healing requires empathy and connection. If Liam learns how to listen to this part of him, he may over time find it easier to say, 'Oh, hey there, self-soother. I know you just want a break from feeling. I hear you and I understand why you want to do that. I know you are trying to help me, but I wonder if there is another way?'

CONTROL AS A PSYCHOLOGICAL PROTECTOR

There are many more patterns of coping we could analyse, but for now let's have a look at this last one: our over-controller coping protector. This is a common one and one that can make parenting feel quite challenging sometimes. This protector is similar to the others and often begins in childhood as a way of helping us to feel safe. It usually stems from unpredictability or from things feeling out of control. It also stems from when a child's emotional needs go unmet and are not soothed by their caregivers. They may learn to hold their feelings inside rather than expressing them. It is influenced by gender roles and cultural norms – for example, 'big boys don't cry' is something many men experienced as young boys growing up. This protector tries its best to suppress our emotions by hiding them or masking our true selves. It is driven by a need for safety and an understandable fear of vulnerability. Let's have a look at Sophie's story.

Sophie grew up in a house with her mom and dad and her younger brother. Sophie's mom and dad unfortunately didn't get on and were always fighting. She remembers feeling quite afraid as a child and never knew what mood to expect her parents to be in. Sophie's mom was experiencing a lot of anxiety in her relationship. She felt like she didn't have control over her life, so in order to compensate for this, she became very controlling of her children. She was critical of Sophie, be it her appearance, how she got on in school or her social circle. Sophie got on well with her dad, but he was quite a passive person and never really listened to Sophie's feelings or stopped her mom from nitpicking her. Sophie's parents were doing the best they could, but they often felt emotionally drained by her.

Sophie was a sensitive child, which meant her stress-response system was quite activated. So unfortunately, when her parents didn't respond to her emotions on a consistent basis, she developed the world view that people cannot be trusted, that she had to be on high alert, and her brain was always scanning for danger. Sophie's parents consistently said things to her when she was a toddler like 'If you won't be good, I'm going to leave you here' when they were out shopping, for example, which set her worried thoughts into overdrive. They would also send her to another room when she was having a tantrum and refuse to speak to her until she calmed down, which worked in the short term to get her to stop but unfortunately sent her the message that they could withdraw their care if she wasn't acting appropriately, making her even more anxious. Over time, Sophie learned that suppressing her needs and her emotions was the safest option. She never cried anymore and hardly ever experienced emotional outbursts. She learned to internalise her pain and rarely expressed her feelings.

Sophie excelled academically. She worked incredibly hard, and achievements meant so much to her. She avoided her emotions by focusing on things she could control, like studying and food. She developed eating difficulties in her teenage years that continued throughout her twenties and thirties, constantly aware of how many calories she was putting in her body along with an obsession with 'clean' foods.

In her late thirties Sophie became a solo parent by choice and conceived her little boy, Conor, via sperm donor. She is completely shaken by how challenging she finds parenting. She becomes obsessed with Conor's routine and follows the baby books she has read perfectly.

Conor sleeps, eats and plays at the same time every day, and Sophie finds that is the only way her anxiety eases. This gives her a sense of control. The difficulty here is that life is always changing, children are unpredictable, and strict routines are hard to follow. So when something unexpected happens in their day, Sophie is consumed with anxiety and feels out of control. Sophie found herself in this situation again recently. She could feel her patience wearing thin. She was looking around at the food on the floor, the endless piles of washing, Conor crying and refusing to go asleep for his scheduled nap, and she burst into tears.

Her punitive pattern of coping is activated in response to feeling vulnerable. She begins to treat Conor in a harsh, punitive manner because that's how she was treated herself. She feels so angry with herself afterwards because she can't make sense of her own responses. 'Why am I so angry?' she asks herself every day.

Feeling overwhelmed like Sophie is understandable as a parent. We are often pulled in so many different directions. Sometimes it feels like we are carrying the weight of the world, along with other life pressures, and it can just feel like too much. On days like these, it feels so much harder to remain calm and regulated. It feels like one more stressful situation is just *too much*. I don't think we talk enough about how understandable it is to reach these points as a parent. Especially parenting sensitive little ones who need that little bit more, which means our own nervous system is going to be activated more, more stressed, more overstimulated.

Please be kind to yourself if you resonate with Sophie's story, and I hope it gives some context to why you might be feeling this way. Similarly to the other stories above, the first step to managing all of this is awareness. Recognise this part of you that needs to feel in control, reflecting on how it shows up in your life. This might sound like: 'I hear you, controller part. I know how routine and structure help you feel safe. It's understandable you feel overwhelmed here.' Sophie likely needs help and support to begin tuning into her own emotions and vulnerability in the context of a safe and supportive relationship. If you resonate with Sophie, linking in with a therapist might be really helpful.

Practical grounding and soothing techniques

These protector parts of us are just trying to support us and have developed to help us. What we want to do is hear them, validate them and hopefully soften them in time so we can begin to feel more connected to ourselves and those around us. The following practical grounding and soothing techniques might be helpful if you are feeling stressed, overwhelmed and in need of a little nervous system reset.

These techniques may be particularly helpful if you begin to notice you are feeling overwhelmed, stressed and reactive or when we are going into a hypoarousal state and zoning out. They can often help ground us in the present moment and help us regulate our nervous system. They can be particularly useful when used as a 'pause' in a challenging situation. With practice this skill supports us to be more intentional about our response and creates space between our emotions and our actions.

GROUNDING TECHNIQUES
- Run cool water over your hands. Hold onto ice cubes if the urge to react is intense.
- Place a cool cloth on your head/face. (Store a hand towel with lavender essential oil in your refrigerator.)
- Grab tightly onto your chair as hard as you can.
- Touch various objects around you: a pen, keys, your clothing, the wall.
- Dig your heels into the floor – literally 'grounding' them! Notice the tension centred in your heels as you do this. Remind yourself you are connected to the ground.
- Carry a grounding object in your pocket that you can touch whenever you feel begin to feel stressed. This can act as a little reminder 'you can do this'.
- Stretch. Roll your head around.
- Clench and release your fists.
- Walk slowly; notice each footstep, saying 'left' or 'right', in detail, to yourself.
- Focus on your breathing: notice each inhale and exhale. Continue for ten slow, deep breaths.
- Scan the room and note five things you see in detail.
- Listen for five things that you can hear – the clock ticking, your own breathing and so on.

- Focus on five things you can feel in contact with your body (for example, your clothes, your back against the chair, your feet on the floor, your hair touching your neck, your watch on your wrist).
- Do the previous three things simultaneously.
- Describe an everyday activity in great detail – for example, getting ready in the morning: 'First I turn on the shower. I then stand in the shower and feel the warm water against my skin. I open my shower gel and squeeze the bottle into my hand. I lather the soap and water and rub my hands against my skin. I close my eyes and smell the scent of the shower gel while I take a few deep breaths.'
- Describe your environment in detail, using all your senses – for example, 'The walls are blue, there are five green chairs, there is a wooden bookshelf against the wall…' Describe objects, sounds, textures, colours, smells, shapes, numbers and temperature. You can do this anywhere.

SELF-SOOTHING TECHNIQUES

These techniques may be particularly helpful if you have gone through a stressful period, if you have had a hard day or have been feeling low or simply as a reminder that you are worthy and that you matter. I really do wish we all remembered to soothe ourselves a little more.

- Get yourself a cup of tea, coffee, juice or water. Drink it slowly, focusing on the sensations of taste, smell and temperature.

- Give yourself a regulating hug: place your right arm across your heart and put your palm against your body with your hand under your armpit. Take your left arm across the body towards the right and hold your shoulder, or upper arm close to your shoulder, for a calming self-hug.
- Wrap yourself in a blanket.
- Wrap yourself in a heated blanket or put your clothes or blanket in the dryer to warm up, then put them on and relax.
- Take a warm shower or bubble bath.
- Play soothing music.
- Burn essential oils in a diffuser.
- Go out into the warm sun for 15 to 30 minutes.
- Practise deep breathing.
- Play, pet (and walk) a pet for 10 minutes or more.
- Engage in rhythmic activities (rocking, walking, running, humming, biking, swimming, dancing).
- Think of the things you're looking forward to in the next week (person you will connect with, activity and so on).
- Think of people you care about and look at pictures of them.
- Say a coping statement – 'I can handle this', 'This feeling will pass'.
- Compassionate self-talk: 'You are doing the best you can. What do you need that might help you feel a little better?'

CHAPTER 5

Temperament, being 'shy' and understanding anxiety

A child with a deep-processing brain that is so perceptive, intuitive and observant is likely to be more cautious and their sensitive nervous system more easily activated than their less-sensitive peers'. A child who is taking in so much from their environment can feel initially apprehensive about new things. It will understandably take a little time to feel comfortable in a novel situation when their nervous system operates with this level of awareness. Imagine noticing every little thing in your surroundings – new faces, new smells, new sounds – all while you are also processing your own feelings and any new sensations, wondering what you make of it all. It makes sense that a child processing this much moves through the world more tentatively.

And it is a *positive* thing to have these little observers in the world. Sensitive children have an internal system known as 'pause to check'. This means that they like to explore a situation by observing and reflecting for a while before they feel comfortable to dive in. This is a great thing in many ways, but unfortunately this way of being in the world can be mislabelled as 'shy' or 'anxious' and begin to be pathologised. We will explore this in further detail below, but I really want to normalise how developmentally appropriate it is for children to want to stay close to their caregivers and how understandable it is to take a little time to warm up in new situations.

Understanding temperament

I wonder if we need to reformulate how we understand anxiety in sensitive children. Of course there are times when our children will experience anxiety, and sometimes they need a little support with this. Often, though, so much of the behaviour we conceptualise as 'anxiety' is actually just part of their temperament. This makes sense in the context of how their nervous system is wired. So often these little observers are more tentative in the world, as they soak in so much information from their environment. Their deep-processing brain then takes some time to process this information, and sometimes our interpretation of this 'pause to check' is that they are anxious. I was speaking to a parent recently who described their little girl as very chatty and fun at home, but she would not talk to strangers, and her childcare providers had observed her to use few words while she was there, despite being engaged with the other children.

If we remember our sensitive children are often cautious and take their time to warm up in new situations, this little girl's behaviour makes sense. We might misinterpret her pensiveness as fragility rather than a wise way in which she is exploring her world. This parent reported her little girl seemed content and at ease, but they were understandably worried she was anxious and wondered how they could support her to be less so in playschool. We might need to trust that they are okay and that their tentative nature does not mean they are feeling fearful. Sometimes our children retreat into themselves even more if they feel under pressure to be different, and this can inadvertently make them more self-conscious about their way of being in the world. If we can, we need to celebrate their strengths and see how powerful and intuitive being this reflective really is.

Sometimes we worry that our children appear 'shy' or 'rude' in the company of others. I have fallen into this trap myself countless times! My children tend to give strangers the 'evil eye' when approached and most definitely will not 'perform' and smile. I have internally winced as a caring older person's kind remarks or attempts to engage them fall flat pretty quickly from two deadpan stares. It really helps to reframe this in the context of their perceptiveness of their environment and their slow-to-warm nature in the world. Our children are often taking time to feel comfortable and are being genuine in not wanting to engage while they pause and take it all in. 'Hmm, who is this lady I have never met before asking me my name? I don't know this person – do my parents? Why are they all staring at me? This is a bit overwhelming. I wish they would stop looking at me ...' They really do just take their time, so try not to worry too much about this.

We often observe our sensitive little souls appearing to be quite 'serious' in new or busy environments, which can sometimes look like they are unhappy, disengaged or disinterested. But if we remember they are soaking in so much internal and external stimuli with such high levels of attunement, then being more 'serious and thoughtful' about it all is a healthy and understandable response. I observed this in one of my children recently. We were at a little graduation show for playschool, and he was so excited to perform in it. When the show started, most of the other children were engaged in the dances and songs while we observed in delight from the audience. My son stood in the middle with a facial expression that alternated between a little smile and a more serious, thoughtful expression and did not engage in the dancing and singing. This could be interpreted as being 'too shy' or that he was anxious. I knew from observing him, and from asking him afterwards about how he was feeling during it, that rather than feeling anxious he was tentatively observing this new situation and perceptively taking in his environment. Lots of new faces to see, along with a whole new routine that day for school, so this made perfect sense to me! 'I loved the show, Mommy! I just liked to stand there, and I danced sometimes. There were so many new people there too. It was so fun – I felt really happy to see you there.' I told him I thought that was really cool and that he did a brilliant job. I could see he was proud of himself, and I was proud of him too. Had I potentially misunderstood his behaviour, I may have said something like: 'Why didn't you join in? Were you too afraid, were you feeling anxious?' and risk him beginning to internalise that he is fearful or 'wrong' in how he conducted himself, despite having felt confident and at ease to be truly himself.

There are times, though, that our sensitive children struggle with anxiety and worries, so let's have a closer look at this. We'll begin with when we first start to see worry or anxiety in our children.

Separation anxiety

Our children are biologically hardwired to be close to us, particularly in the first few years when our attachment relationships are forming and deepening. This is a great thing, and it is a normal, healthy part of their development. The onset of focused attachment is usually around six to ten months (timelines vary, as every child is unique). This is usually when we see a strong preference for one caregiver emerge and what is known as 'separation anxiety' – distress on being apart from that person. This person tends to be the one who is the most active in the child's care. Through consistent and reliable responding from this caregiver, the baby learns they can depend on them to meet their needs. The primary caregiver is particularly important for the first few months, as small babies physically need our presence to help regulate their heart rate and breathing systems and let us know when they are hungry, tired, seeking comfort, in pain and so on. Our attunement, responsiveness and love help our baby's brain fire and wire neural connections that build the foundations of secure attachment, like safety and trust. For this reason, it really is impossible to spoil a baby!

A little later, when toddlers feel safe and secure in the relationship with their primary caregiver, they begin to explore other relationships. They have developed an internal representation of this person, which then gives them the confidence to develop and build other connections. What we often see during this stage, when the toddler begins to exercise their autonomy, is a shift in parental preference. This can take some parents by surprise and can evoke strong feelings in us. Depending on our own life history, it is not unusual for it to activate feelings of abandonment or rejection. If this is something you are experiencing, try to remember it is all very normal – and it's actually a great sign that they feel secure in their relationship with you. Similarly, if you are not seeing this, do not panic, as all children are individuals, and these developmental stages will look different for every child. Sometimes the parental preference stays strong with the primary caregiver throughout, and this is just part of their unique development.

Separation anxiety tends to peak again around 14 to 18 months, around age 3 and during transitions like starting school, the addition of a new sibling or any other change in their life. Our more sensitive children may have a more difficult time with this, as they are feeling their emotions so deeply. I would love parents of these children to know that it is *not* their fault. So many parents I work with believe they have done something wrong to cause this separation anxiety in their child, when often this is a very healthy and developmentally appropriate response. And it is not something we need to pathologise either. They are only small, and it's understandable for them to want to remain connected to us. Many other factors may impact their separation anxiety as they get older, such as feeling left out in school, not getting along with their teacher, feeling worried about tests, finding the learning a challenge, feeling sick, tired, hungry. At times of stress or change, it is normal to see separation anxiety increase again and for them to seek more reassurance as a way of creating safety. Try not to worry that it means they will be anxious forever – hold on to the knowledge that independence from us comes from meeting their need for dependence, and these periods of connection-seeking with us make perfect sense!

I often see conflicting information on this, particularly when we view a child's behaviour through a purely behavioural lens. Some people believe that if we continue to support our children around times of heightened anxiety, then we are negatively reinforcing their behaviour. While this may be true in some cases, this advice often does not take temperament into account and does not value just how important it is to help our children feel understood. It also does not account for how appropriate it is that they will seek this connection sometimes. We have so much research now to support the fact that pushing a child before they are ready does not foster resilience. We should lean in and support them during times of connection-seeking and help them feel safe, and then gently encourage the separation again when they feel ready. Again, this is complex, as it is often a careful balance between meeting them where they are at *and* empowering them to go outside their comfort zone.

Sometimes, if we are feeling anxious ourselves, we might inadvertently maintain their anxiety because we don't want them to feel the way we do. So, for example, we might say, 'Okay, don't worry, you don't have to go to football – I don't want you to do things that make you feel stressed'. We mean well when we do this, but often the scary situation becomes bigger in their minds when avoidance becomes a pattern. We might say instead, 'Aw, I know you are worried about it, love. I completely understand. Why don't we go together and stay for five minutes and see how you feel then?' Most likely, once our child is immersed in the activity, they will realise the worry about it was scarier than being there. Of course, this won't always be the case, and sometimes it really will be too much for them. This will look different for every child and involves a little trial and error on our part. But the main message we always want to give is that we understand it is scary or we understand that they are worried *and* that we believe in them. The more we meet their need for safety and security, the more confident they will feel without us, rather than the opposite being true. It also helps their trust in us to wire in deeply. They learn they can depend on us or confide in us with their worries.

LEAVING YOUR SENSITIVE CHILD IN CHILDCARE
I know this can be difficult to manage. Recently I had a heart-wrenching drop-off at my son's playschool. He loves it there and we are incredibly lucky with how kind, warm and nurturing the staff are. This was a really important consideration for us when we were trying to figure out what playschool he would go to. I knew it would take patience and time for him to feel safe in a new environment at such a young age. We visited the playschool

on many occasions and got to know his teacher, while she kindly let me stay and play for the duration. We collaborated on a very slow, gradual transition in, whereby I would stay and play for 40 minutes and then leave for 10, slowly building it up so that he would stay for the whole morning. This worked really well and despite always being cautious at first, he would often go in happily in the end. This journey has not been linear, though, with plenty of days being a little too much sometimes.

Despite loving playschool now and forming such close bonds with his amazing childcare educators, there are still times he just wants to be at home. This is frequently the case with the primary caregiver – their separation anxiety peaks with us – but it is usually nothing to worry about: remember, it is in the closest relationships that children feel safe enough to show their true feelings. My poor big-hearted little guy was so upset outside his classroom door recently at drop-off – despite his kind teacher's best efforts, he clung to me and begged me to bring him home. On a different day, had I not had deadlines and work commitments, I would have brought him home and had a relaxing morning with him, understanding he just needed a bit of connection with me, but this day, I had deadlines and work commitments.

I can't say I skipped away unfazed after his teacher gave him a big hug and carried him crying in the door. My heart broke watching his little face crumple and plead to come with me. Tears rolled down my face the whole way home, as I felt so guilty for leaving him while he was upset. I received a video five minutes later from his teacher that showed him happily playing with her and laughing and joking into the camera. This eased my guilt a little, but it is so hard to navigate this, and I have so much compassion for parents who have to do this all the time.

I am aware how privileged I was to be able to slowly get my son used to his playschool. Being self-employed then, I could make the time to help the transition happen as smoothly as possible. I know this just isn't the reality for so many families, and not everyone can take time off work or has enough resources to help. I have worked with the kindest parents who feel guilty about this, as they fear they are not doing the best thing for their child yet have no other option. I reassure these parents that the research on childcare shows that parent and family characteristics are more strongly linked to child development than childcare is. 'Family features matter more' when it comes to predicting outcomes, meaning how we are in our relationship with our children influences their development more than the hours they are in childcare. This does not mean that childcare is insignificant – they can learn so much from being in a childcare setting and often form beautiful bonds with their childcare providers. But it is comforting for parents to know that, at the end of the day, the parent–child relationship is the most influential. If you are worrying about this, please try to remember that and also that we can only do our best with the resources we have. Sometimes the environment may not be the right fit for your sensitive child, particularly if it operates from a less nurturing approach or if the child is experiencing significant stress due to the separation. This will be individual to each child and family circumstances, so if it is something you are concerned about, reaching out to a child therapist for individualised support and guidance through this process would be really helpful.

Separating from us will often cause our more sensitive souls stress. This stress makes so much sense (we are their safe place) and usually will not be damaging for them longer term, once they are being soothed and looked after by someone who cares about them. A big question to consider asking childcare providers is how they respond to a child who is upset. Do they comfort and soothe them, or do they leave them alone to process their feelings? How stressed a child is while coping with the transition to childcare may be drastically different depending on this answer. In an ideal world, we really want the childcare setting to be another nurturing, warm and attuned relationship our child has in their life. And, of course, there are also times our children just want to be with us, and it is not stemming from fear or anxiety. They may just want some more connection and comfort from us, as my son did.

Understanding big emotions after school

You might be wondering why your child seems to be experiencing so many big feelings when they come home from school. Sometimes our sensitive children hold all their emotions in while they are there, and we see a big release when they are finally home with their safe person and feel comfortable enough to release all of the big feelings they were trying to manage all day. We might observe this in the form of tantrums, meltdowns and lots of tears. It is not necessarily a cause for concern and is often an appropriate way of processing their emotions or an understandable physiological response from feeling exhausted, particularly when they have spent a period of time without their safe person! Our sensitive children have spent a long time 'being good' and thus have nothing left in the tank when they are home, and the stored-up frustrations, upset and overstimulation from the day are finally given space to flow out. This makes sense, but that does not mean it is easy to manage as a parent. It can be challenging when the behaviour is often that of anger towards you – shouting, hitting, throwing. We also need to be mindful that if this behaviour is happening continuously, and our child appears to be more stressed in general – maybe we see their separation anxiety increase hugely or they are fighting with peers and siblings or no longer playing independently – then perhaps this is an indication that they need support and some adaptations to their environment.

This behaviour could also be a defensive response to being reunited with their safe person. I still remember the 'bad moods' I had towards my own caregivers after school when I was small. I would respond defensively and often 'rudely' to them, while inside I felt overwhelmed from my day and was seeking connection and a gentle understanding. I am observing this in my youngest at the moment. When I come home, he initially looks so relieved to see my face, but what sometimes follows this is an angry response. He comes over and shakes his head at me and says, 'Hit you, Mommy.' You may see this kind of response in your older child if you collect them from school and they say unkind things to you or appear to be rude or angry. Often, they have just spent much of their day managing different emotions and situations without your soothing presence, so it is understandable that they may feel initially angry with you while they process the separation from you. It can be so easy to take this personally, and I don't always get it right either! If you can, though, try and let this behaviour go and meet it with loving kindness instead. What is being communicated under the anger is often 'I missed you', 'I needed you', 'You left me'. If we meet this need with understanding and empathy, the behaviour will usually soften in response. It also communicates to your child that you see them, that you love them and that you understand. I can't emphasise enough how helpful empathy for our children in these moments will be for deepening our connection with them.

A GENTLE PUSH TO THE EDGE OF THEIR WINDOW OF TOLERANCE

It's important to really hear our kids when they tell us how they are feeling, but equally, sometimes they need our help to push them a little outside their comfort zone. Due to their sensitive nervous system, they may seek to choose the more comfortable option during times of worry. If we think back to the window of tolerance, we know that sometimes theirs is a little more sensitive to overwhelm. As they grow and are learning new skills, starting big school, then secondary school, and doing things that feel understandably scary for the first time, our goal is to help push them to the edge of this window. This is called the optimal zone of tolerance. It means they are not so stressed that their threat response has been activated, but they may feel slight discomfort and worry. However, while they might feel initially uncertain and uncomfortable, pushing themselves to 'feel the fear and do it anyway' is how they learn a sense of mastery in different situations or when learning new skills.

This is where it all gets complicated – when we try to understand fear and sensitivity. On the one hand, it is important to be child-led and really hear our children when they say things feel 'too much' or that they need a break. Where possible, it is brilliant to validate their needs, and if that means they need a day off school or activities, it is a great little nervous-system reset. On the other hand, it is not uncommon for our sensitive souls to get stuck in little worry loops that become bigger and bigger in their head. So what might start off as a little whisper of 'I want to stay home with my mom/dad today' can turn into 'I don't like school', 'I don't like my teachers', 'I don't have any friends'.

We know our own child best, and often we can tell the difference in how stressed our child appears to be. I know my child's cry and expression of 'No, Mom, I don't want to go today', but with the ability to 'feel the fear and do it anyway', as opposed to his very distressed cry where his face goes red and he finds it hard to breathe – 'Please, don't leave me here'. There is an important distinction between these two patterns. Learning occurs when we are still within our window of tolerance but being pushed to the uncomfortable edge of this. Our child may feel stressed and upset initially but does the scary thing anyway, and this builds confidence over time. Unfortunately, learning does not occur when we are so distressed that we shut down. This is so hard for parents when we have no option other than to go to work, so please remember we are all just doing the best we can. If we have

TEMPERAMENT, BEING 'SHY' AND UNDERSTANDING ANXIETY

no option but to leave our child when they are distressed, then leaving them in a nurturing environment with empathic childcare providers will be a big help.

Another factor that makes separation from our children hard for us to navigate as parents is when we consider how vocal our sensitive little ones can be. They often wear their heart on their sleeve and can be very expressive with their emotions. They also *feel* their emotions so intensely. So for the 30 seconds they feel scared or sad, they feel it times 100! And then 30 seconds after that they might realise they are okay and actually going into school or to the activity is 'no big deal'. This always involves a little trial and error while we figure out what is best for our child.

> *Aisling went through a period of intense separation anxiety from ages six through eight. Trying to get her to go to school was always stressful for her parents, as her little deep-processing mind decided every morning at the school door that she just wanted to go home. When Aisling felt at ease and her parents asked her why she was so upset in the mornings, she also felt confused by her own behaviour. She loved her class, had lots of friends and always enjoyed her day once she was there. Yet every morning, the same distress would happen, and she would beg to come home. In hindsight, she most likely needed a few more breaks throughout the year, and a mental health day here and there would have been a big help (though not always possible or realistic for working families, I know!). It all only started to shift when she realised herself*

that she could feel overwhelmed with one emotion one minute and then overwhelmed by another emotion the next. Her nervous system began to understand and remember, 'Oh yeah, this happens, but I will most likely be okay once I am in there'. Her parents helped her with this in several ways:

- *They modelled calm, showing confidence and demonstrating that they heard her.*
- *They let her know her feelings made sense: 'It's hard going into school sometimes, pet, I know. I remember it so well too. I used to love staying at home in my favourite place. I get it.'*
- *They practised deep-breathing exercises together, like taking big sighs and pretending to blow up a big balloon.*
- *They reminded her how this happened every day and once she was in there she felt okay. They asked Aisling to close her eyes and visualise her day in school, focusing on her friends, the nice lunch she has packed, the games she will play on her break and so on.*
- *They visualised what would happen when Aisling came home and just how excited they would be to see her after school.*
- *Finally, they used positive affirmations: 'You've got this, love! I believe in you.'*

Sometimes we need a little 'bridge' that helps our sensitive kids take those leaps they are worried about. One that helped Aisling at the time was knowing that if things felt like they were 'too much', she could ask her teacher to ring her parents and someone would come to take her home. We want them to see that we really believe in them, but equally we are here for them if they need us. Having that safety blanket in the back of their mind can be extremely helpful. They might never use it, but just knowing it is there and that they have the support of someone who loves them and sees them is hugely beneficial. Some people reading this may be thinking that if they gave that option, they would be being called to collect their child all the time. You know your own child best, and if that bridging sounds too open-ended, have a think of others that might help. It could be a special notebook that you give them each morning with a little 'I believe in you' note, letting them know how much you love them and outlining all the nice things you can't wait to do with them when they are home. Or drawing a heart on their wrist and yours to remind them that you are always carrying them in your heart and that you can't wait to see them after school.

Worries and the sensitive child

Worries and a sensitive little soul often go hand in hand, as we live in a fast-paced and overwhelming world. When you have a child with a soft heart and a reflective, deep-thinking brain, it's not unusual for their empathy to lead them to feel concerned about the well-being of their family, friends, animals and other people in the world. I cover this in more depth in chapters six and eight. If we remember our sensitive children often need a little more time, then we can understand how they might worry about their day if they are overstimulated, and life is moving too quickly. Sometimes, when we reduce the overwhelming stimuli by slowing down their day or routine, we may see a softening of their worries. This will involve a bit of trial and error on our part, but let the worries be a guide that something in the environment needs adapting.

I always say to parents, 'Let worry be your invitation into your child's way of telling us they are experiencing big feelings'. It is more often than not their way of letting us know they need more connection and need our comforting presence to help them feel safe again. When our child's body is in their threat system, their brain often comes up with a reason for the alarm they are feeling inside. We can see this when our child is worried about things like monsters, ghosts and other scary characters from their imagination. Our inclination is often to dismiss the worry – 'Oh, they are not real! You have nothing to be afraid of.' This is understandable; we want our children to feel okay. If you can, though, try and remember that it is not necessarily about the 'monster' per se, but rather their way of communicating to you that their body does not feel at ease, and they need to be soothed.

So while we know monsters aren't real, monsters can *feel* real in our imaginations. It can be helpful instead to be curious about their worry: 'Oh, love, you saw a monster? How did that make you feel?' 'I felt scared!' 'You poor pet, you felt scared. I am here, love. Let me give you a big hug.' We want to validate the feeling by letting them know we hear them, and we understand. We might gently investigate what the fear is. 'What is the scariest part about the monster, love?' 'They are really big, and they are coming to get me.' We can continue to remain empathic and curious with them: 'Oh, that certainly sounds scary. I can see why you feel that way.' There are so many ways we can then help our child feel soothed. We can tell friendly monster stories and help them understand that, while it makes sense that they feel real, monsters are characters from stories and are a part of our imagination. We can reorient them to the safety of their environment, helping ground them in the present with our comfort and some of their comfort items. Play is a fantastic way we can help our children move through worries, allowing them release anxious feelings in their body, feel empowered and more in control. We can do our best to tune into our own playful side – 'Oh, hey, monster! I am even *bigger* than you! You don't stand a chance against me,' or zooming around the room on a pretend broom, for example. The main message you are sending to your child is 'I am here. You are safe. You are loved.' Be as silly as you can too! We want our children to join with us in this and feel like they are gaining mastery and developing their bravery and courage. Your child might pretend to be a huge lion and roar towards the corners of the room. My son, at the moment, turns into the Hulk while we 'banish all the baddies' in the hallway when the uncertainty of the dark begins to fall. This can help so much on a physiological level by gently releasing the tension of worry from their bodies.

Think about your own experience of worries. Do you find it hard sometimes to 'resolve' a worry? Or when you are going through a challenging time and trying your best to push down painful emotions, do you notice worry loops becoming difficult to manage? Worries are often a powerful coping protector that manifest when we feel scared, sad or like we are not good enough. So sometimes, rather than getting caught up in the cognitive content of worries, it helps to go straight to the underlying need our child might be inadvertently communicating. That need is often to feel safe, loved, validated, accepted and understood.

Our child's worries can also manifest in other ways if they are feeling anxious about something like school, for example. We may think they are doing okay yet all of a sudden notice they are experiencing toilet regressions, nightmares, stomach problems and so on. When this happens, we need to help our children feel safe again in their body, remembering that worries are often letting us know that our child is experiencing stress. And the best way to help our children with this is to increase our empathy and our connection. The most powerful way to move worries through our own bodies and our child's is through movement and play. However, if your child's worries are significantly impacting their day-to-day, this may be a sign they need some support from a therapist or psychologist.

FIGHT/FLIGHT/FREEZE/FAWN RESPONSE

Our brain responds to threats in a variety of ways. Imagine being out for a walk in a beautiful woodland area and you come across a lion. Immediately adrenaline and cortisol are released in your body. Your airwaves open up, your pupils dilate, and your heart starts beating really fast. Your brain is preparing you to either fight that lion or run as fast as you possibly can (flight). But let's say we know we can't get away. We know we can't outrun the lion, and we don't have the physical strength to fight it. In this case, our brain and body prepare themselves for injury. Our heart rate slows down, and we psychologically dissociate and disengage. This is called our freeze response. You may have heard of the fawn response too. This is a more recent addition to our understanding of trauma and survival responses and is when a human or animal engages in appeasing or pleasing behaviour to protect themselves from experiencing harm. It involves compliance at the cost of the person's own needs and is an extremely adaptive coping mechanism in stressful and abusive situations.

WHEN THEIR MIND BECOMES OVERPROTECTIVE

Sometimes, depending on their environment or new skills they are learning, our sensitive child's mind may be a little overprotective. Their threat system might be working that little bit too hard, and we may need to help them with this. As a parent, knowing that it is understandable to have more worries if you feel the world deeply makes it a lot easier to help our children manage. We can be their biggest supporters when we know that their worries are likely stemming from that big heart of theirs that cares so much.

It is not unusual for our child to ask us, 'What is wrong with me?' if they notice they are more fearful than others in a situation. And our reflexive answer may be to say, 'Nothing is wrong with you, love!' because we want them to feel okay, and we don't want them to feel any different. However, a child who feels so deeply may already have noticed that they experience the world a little differently to their peers. So unfortunately, while we mean well, telling them there is nothing wrong may unintentionally invalidate their experience and leave them feeling confused.

What is hugely powerful instead is to help them understand what is happening for them. Although we might not see results straight away, this helps them learn how to manage anxiety as they grow. They begin to understand the way their brain works and why they feel anxious sometimes. They learn that they are in control of their body, rather than their body being in control of them. This helps them feel more confident in handling scary situations or worries they experience.

> *Síofra is an eight-year-old who is going back to school after her midterm break. She is a sensitive child who is naturally quiet and gentle and is a big observer of her environment. When she is around close friends and family, she feels at ease, but she can find school a little difficult sometimes. Her peers are quite a lively bunch, so often she finds it hard to speak up. This can result in Síofra feeling like she doesn't really fit in. Her parents feel sad that she is having a hard time and are unsure how to help her. They notice she hasn't been sleeping well in the lead-up to returning to school, and she is expressing how much she doesn't want to go. She wakes up on the first day back explaining that she is dreading yard time and has a pain in her tummy.*

This can be so hard to navigate, and I have worked with many kind parents who feel heartbroken watching their child struggle.

One idea that might help here is for Síofra's parents to help her understand her 'worry brain'.

> 'I am so sorry you are worried, pet; it makes so much sense that you feel nervous about going back to school. I know that feeling well too. Often when we have a little break from something we feel worried about, our worry gets bigger and bigger in our mind. We all have a little alarm system in our brain where our worries live. This alarm system is always trying to protect us and keep us safe. For some of us with big hearts that feel everything deeply, our alarms can work a bit too hard. This is not our fault at all – the alarm just gets a little confused sometimes and tells us we are in danger when we might actually be okay. We can do lots of things to help this and learn how to figure out what is a real alarm and what is a false alarm.'

The first thing to show Síofra are in-the-moment strategies to help her feel more at ease. Síofra's parent's teach her to:

- Become a curious detective about her thoughts and feelings. When she starts to feel worried, they teach her to say, 'Oh, hey, worry! I hear you and I hear that little alarm going off.'
- Begin noticing what her bodily sensations feel like. She learns there is a pain in her tummy and that it feels harder to breathe when worry is here. They teach her how to breathe a little

easier by taking a big deep breath and a big exhale, like she's doing a big sigh or blowing out all the candles on a cake.
- Ground herself by feeling her feet on the floor and then to look around and name five things she can see, four things she can hear, three things she can touch, two things she can smell and one thing she can taste.
- Use her body to regulate her emotions by humming, swaying and giving herself a big deep-pressure hug.

These strategies can be hard to access when we are overwhelmed because we lose access to our thinking, rational brain. So the more Síofra practises these when she feels calm and at ease, the easier it will become for her to access them when her worries feel really big.

The next step – helping Síofra to plan ahead or navigate these tricky situations in school – involves a little trial and error. Of course her parents want to fix it and take her worry away. But sometimes our best option is to validate her experience and help her to recognise the pressure she might be putting herself under to be as loud as the others or to participate in some yard activity that she finds overwhelming. If Síofra can continue learning how she feels and how to mind herself in these situations, it may become easier for her to tune into what she really needs. Her parents suggest that, instead of trying to be part of the big group, she take the pressure off and ask one person she gets on with to play or chat. Her parents remind her that it's understandable her worry pops up at these times and that they believe in her. They leave a little note in her copy every morning telling her how proud they are of her and what a special person she is. When she comes home from school, they listen as best they can about her day and try their best to really hear her and be a kind and non-judgemental listening ear. They remind themselves that their goal is not to fix this for her but to be there for her and help her feel understood. A really difficult part of parenting is being able to step back and trust that things will be okay. Our support and compassion during the challenges our children face growing up help wire their brain to do this for themselves over time.

TEACHING CHILDREN TO BE CURIOUS ABOUT COPING PROTECTORS

It can be a good idea to sit down with our children and figure out what kind of 'protectors' they use to keep themselves safe. These protectors are things we all do to try to keep us from experiencing the things we are scared of. For a child who worries about going to school, their little protector might be to pretend they are sick in order to stay home instead. For a child who worries about being left alone at a sleepover, their protector might be to ring their parent to pick them up. For a child who worries about being sick, their protector might be to avoid certain foods. For a child who worries about germs, their protector might be to wash their hands repeatedly throughout the day. For a child who worries about crowds, their protector might be to never go to busy places. For a child who worries about not fitting in, their protector might be to sit alone and not engage with peers. For a child who worries about not playing well in a football match, their protector might be to pretend their foot is sore, and the list goes on.

Here is where it all gets a little complicated again. What we always want to do is really listen to them and believe their worry is real. And we know that worries can manifest as pains in our body and nausea, so if they are saying they feel sick, it's important to listen to that! We also know that our more sensory-sensitive children will find certain foods difficult, crowds too overwhelming, school too much sometimes and so on. So I am not suggesting we ignore that, and this is where understanding your child's sensory profile (see chapter ten) will be a helpful guide. But here, let's assume that what they are experiencing is a worry, rather than a sensory need.

For example, maybe your child is feeling worried about starting a new sport. They are saying, 'My arm is too sore – I won't be able to play tennis today. I slept on it funny, and I know I won't be able to play.' You could then sit down with your child and be curious with them about how their worry shows up – remembering first and foremost to empathise with feeling afraid of trying something new. 'I completely get it, pet. I remember the worry I would feel before starting something new. That makes so much sense. Sometimes once we give it a shot we find we actually really like it. Often the thought of doing it is worse than when we are there. Why don't we just turn up and try it today – no pressure, let's just see how it goes?'

Our goal is to teach them to slowly move towards those things that make them afraid. This is because, while these little protectors do a great job of keeping us safe in the moment, they often prolong our worries overall. When our child engages in their protector for too long, the message that wires into their nervous system is 'Phew, okay, we are safe because we used our protector, and we didn't have to do the scary thing.' This makes them less likely to do the feared thing again in the future. So the hard part for our kids here is that they need to expose themselves to the scary situation to help send the message to their brain that it's okay. Repeated patterns of this over time help them feel more confident in themselves and help the worry to ease.

One thing that I find useful when working with these wonderful children is to help them draw pictures of their worry brain. If your child has seen *Inside Out*, the Disney Pixar movie, you might think of this character too. Or they might pick a little character from the toy shop that reminds them of their worry brain. This step is important because we need to teach them that their worry is a part of them, but it's not all of them. We need to help them externalise the worry and create a little distance from it so they can challenge it. Play is a fantastic way of doing this with our children, and we can set up a scenario like a tea party where we invite worry along for tea. We can pull up a seat and say, 'Hey, worry! You are so busy in there coming up with lots of things to be scared about. I know you're only trying to help, but it can be a bit of a pain sometimes. Thank you for helping, worry, but I've got this.'

The 'shy' child

When we think about 'shyness', we often worry this means our children are really anxious and lacking in confidence. This is because being an 'extravert' is often praised in our society and 'shyness' looked at through a negative lens. Before we examine what being shy really means, let us look at the complexities of introversion and extraversion to help us make sense of this.

Introversion and extraversion exist along a continuum – we are all unique, so usually none of us will fit neatly into any category! For the most part, though, the research shows us that roughly 70 per cent of highly sensitive people identify with the trait of introversion. Introverts often find strength and energy from being alone and may find things like group work or social gatherings difficult. The other 30 per cent of sensitive people are extraverts. This means they get a lot of energy from other people and often thrive in social environments. Too much time alone can lead them to feel down, lethargic and unmotivated. This is important to reflect on for ourselves and our kids because it helps us learn what they need. We don't need to push an introverted child to be an extravert! This happens frequently and unfortunately sends the message over time that they are not okay as who they are. Instead, we can celebrate their strengths as introverts and recognise we don't need to push them to be different.

You might also have a child who is an extravert. I always wondered why, when I love being around people and feel so fulfilled with others, I feel so depleted afterwards and need time alone. I used to refer to myself as an introverted extravert. Dr Elain Aron has explained how extraverts get their energy renewed by spending time with people and introverts get their energy renewed by spending time alone to process and think about ideas, and to participate in quiet, more thoughtful activities. She then asks the question 'What about the sensitive extravert?' Unlike the sensitive introvert, we go inward (i.e. we introvert) mainly to

TEMPERAMENT, BEING 'SHY' AND UNDERSTANDING ANXIETY

recover, rest and renew – not necessarily because we prefer to be alone. After our physical and mental energies are recharged by being 'in', we go 'out' to manifest our visions, our passions and our work to the world.

You might identify with this or recognise this in your child. The problem is that even though the extravert in us might be gaining a lot from the external world, our nervous system is processing so much information that we can become overstimulated and overwhelmed more easily. This is why we can switch from really enjoying a social occasion to very quickly feeling exhausted and depleted in energy. I love being in social settings and feel so energised by others, but when this happens, I can only describe it like 'hitting a wall', and any conversation afterwards takes a huge amount of energy. It helps to understand this so we can recognise when our children, or indeed ourselves, need a nervous system reset!

Whether your child is an introvert or a sensitive extravert, you might be wondering if they are 'shy' and why they don't just jump in to social settings in the same way their peers do. These children are processing their environment deeply, so it makes sense that they are often more cautious, perceptive and tentative. They are noticing all the subtleties, all of the little things that others might miss. They often like to sit back and observe their surroundings before they feel comfortable enough to dive in. The language and understanding we have here will make a huge difference for them in how we interpret their behaviour and how they learn to make sense of their own. Unfortunately, 'shyness' is viewed negatively in many cultures with parents believing they need to make their child less shy and bolder. Let's untangle this a little. Temperamental shyness is observed in people and animals and generally refers to a tendency for behavioural inhibition (e.g. withdrawing) in novel situations. Research finds that shyness can be associated with anxiety later in life. While some sensitive children do show behavioural inhibition in novel situations (pause to check), once they have paused to check, their strategy might be a bold one or a cautious one. Sensitivity may overlap with shyness, but as we have discussed, sensitivity is not fearfulness. A sensitive child may be bold, confident and extraverted or they may be cautious and introverted. If you have a younger child, you can practise building their confidence and self-esteem by showing them it's okay to take your time. Your response to someone who comments on how shy they are might be: 'They are actually just taking their time! My little observer here just likes to suss the scene out before diving in.' You might narrate for your child what you think they are experiencing: 'Oh, wow, it's a big party here today. I can imagine you are just taking it all in, love – that's okay! It's normal to take your time. I am right here and there's no rush. I've got you.' You might then spend time saying, 'Oh, cool, look at what that child is playing with! I wonder should we go over and say hello?' We need to remind ourselves that they often require a little more time, and we should go a little slower if we can, trusting that when they feel safe enough, they will feel more confident to explore. That safety comes from their trusting in us, that we are there for them and that we understand. I know many parents find this really challenging, having received judgemental comments from others about their child's 'shyness' and how mollycoddling them is not doing them any favours.

> Jack is a father to a sensitive child named Paul. Paul, now nearing the end of primary school (age 12), is still his sensitive-natured 'shy and quiet' self. Jack always valued his son's gentle temperament and never pushed him to be different, although he also hoped Paul would become 'louder' and more confident as he grew. We spoke about this at the time, and I reminded him that confidence does not mean extraversion. True confidence comes from knowing deep down at your core that you are a worthy person, and you are loveable as you are. We can be confident and quiet, and being 'shy' is not a negative thing. Jack began to receive a lot of judgement from well-intentioned family and friends about his son and how he would manage in secondary school. They feared Paul was the way he was because Jack had 'mollycoddled' him, and he should have pushed him more. They believed he was 'too soft' on him and that it was his fault his son was not thriving in social environments and was not the 'leader of the pack'.
>
> As a result of this, this kind father had begun to push Paul to be more resilient by being tougher on him at home. He started to believe, 'Well, if I am harder on him now here, then at least he will know what to expect in school. Boys can be cruel.' It made so much sense why Jack started treating Paul this way. He loved him so much and couldn't

bear the thought of him being bullied in school or taken advantage of by others. So he thought, 'I'll teach him here and build up his resilience.' Unfortunately Jack and Paul's relationship became strained and, though previously they'd been so close, Paul withdrew from Jack and began exhibiting signs of depression.

While Jack's behaviour is understandable, we now know that the number-one predictor of a child's resilience, which gives them a buffer against life's challenges, is the quality of the relationship with their attachment figures. I worked with Jack, empathising with the situation and helping him to observe Paul through the lens of his being a deep-feeling child with a huge heart that needs warmth, kindness and love to build his self-worth. Jack spent time repairing his relationship with Paul, apologising for the way he had been treating him and letting Paul know that he loves him just as he is. They spent more time together, and Paul no longer exhibited any signs of depression and went back to being his unique and wonderful self.

Life can be painful and, unfortunately, we can't completely shield children from being bullied, being excluded, not fitting in, feeling different. But the one thing we do have within our control is how we respond to them. We can try our best to remain as consistent as possible in our approach to helping them navigate these challenges. We can tune into the anxiety, sadness, fear and shame that this evokes in us from our own childhood wounds. We can soothe our stress response and remind ourselves that it's okay for our child to have these big feelings and it's okay that it's hard for us too. We can lean into them with kindness and compassion, soothing our own pain of not being able to take it away, while listening and validating their pain. We need to believe that we don't have to teach them how to be resilient. Life's mixture of joy and suffering will do that on its own The number-one buffer in helping them navigate it all and in building true resilience is a foundation of love and acceptance from us.

One of the biggest gifts we can give our children is loving and accepting them for who they are.

CHAPTER 6

The empath

As the parent of a child with big feelings, I'm sure you feel a little worn out sometimes. Even the most empathic of us may feel stretched thin with helping our children manage the swirl of emotions inside. I hope this chapter will help you understand the mind of an empathic child and provide you with some practical tips on how to help them.

Growing up as an empath

When I was a child, I felt so different sometimes. It was like I had some kind of magical antenna that was picking up on all of the energy and emotions around me. I would not only notice someone's mood, but I could also *physically feel* their mood. This was fantastic if the people around me were experiencing joy or giving off energy that felt warm inside. Their excitement, love or happiness pulled me into their energy zone, and I felt immediately uplifted. My emotions, posture and facial expression would begin to mirror theirs. I know that probably sounds strange if this doesn't happen to you too. I used to describe feeling like I had no skin sometimes, that all of my feelings were dancing around outside my body. I read a beautiful book recently by Cecelia Ahern called *In a Thousand Different Ways*, and it's such an insightful look into the mind of a sensitive person.

I can't pretend this magical antenna always felt that great. I would also pick up and physically feel someone's not-so-helpful mood. This was a huge challenge for me throughout my life and something I feel passionate about helping sensitive children and adults with now. I seemed to lack the ability to separate someone's mood and behaviour from mine. I believed this was because I was 'too sensitive' and took everything personally. I always hated this about myself and felt like it made me sound neurotic and self-centred. Was I really just making everything about myself?

The answer was yes and no. Yes, in that I was a very sensitive child, and like all children I had a deep need to feel understood, loved, accepted and valued. And because I was a child that had a more sensitive nervous system, a little alarm would signal quickly if there was any perceived threat. Feeling ignored or dismissed felt like a real threat to my survival. Therefore, I was highly attuned when someone's mood shifted and worried it was because of me. All children are egocentric – they tend to internalise everything. This is developmentally appropriate and is how they make sense of the world. So in that way I was definitely operating from a more self-focused perspective, one that had difficulty questioning other hypotheses that may have been in play – one being that maybe someone else's mood switch had nothing to do with me! A thought, I am sad to say, that rarely ever entered my head.

And then there is the no. This is where understanding the empath's mind is crucial in helping them navigate the world. Their brain chemistry is wired so that their mirror neuron response system is firing away much more frequently than those of us who are not as empathic. That magical antenna of theirs is so incredibly strong that it can be hard to protect their own energy. Thanks to their very active complex neurobiology and nervous system, they can get sucked into what feel like dark holes in someone's energy zone. They often physically feel others' emotions. I remember how a close person's agitated sigh or curt reply in conversation would feel like a punch in the stomach. One of my friends at the time could be a little moody (can't we all!). This was not their fault – we can thank hormones and just being a kid for that! I loved being around them so much, but when their mood switched, I was always taken aback how quickly I moved from feeling warm and happy to feeling like a deflating balloon. I would often feel like I was watching myself in a movie as time slowed down and the air would deflate painfully slowly as my feelings changed. I would feel heavy and sad. It is difficult to describe how disappointed you feel inside when this happens – a deep knowing that your day has drastically changed. That little antenna of mine would jump into fixer mode, wondering what happened. What was wrong? Did I do something? But none of us usually get clear answers to these questions, if we can even ask them, and there begins the exhausting journey of contemplating what went wrong. And trying to do that while feeling agitated and frustrated, unsure where your feelings start and the other's end. Whose annoyance is this? The confusing swirl happening inside feels so uncomfortable and deflating.

One of the most challenging aspects of this is trying to shake off someone else's mood – or, indeed, to shake off our own not-so-helpful mood. If you have a little empath, chances are they are experiencing a whole range of emotions every day. We want to teach them that all emotions are okay. They are all little messengers of information, always guiding us towards something that we need.

Many of us have grown up believing that anger is wrong and sadness is weak. So, thanks to our powerful protectors, we have learned how to push it down. Sadly, that has impacted many of us today, as our repressed emotions have found other avenues to leak out. This often leaves us confused and unsure of our behaviour and emotional responses. This is where we can empower our children and model that emotions like anger and sadness are important! Anger helps guide us towards something that doesn't feel right. A boundary has been crossed or a need is being missed. Sadness is guiding us towards something that feels hurt, a part of us that needs comfort and tender care.

Something that can be quite complex for our sensitive kids is that, due to their deep-processing brains, it is not unusual for them to find themselves stuck in their emotions and feel a little 'moody'. Shaking off an unhelpful mood can be a real challenge. There are a few reasons why and some things to be aware of while we are parenting little empaths. Before reading this, please go easy on yourselves! We don't know what we don't know, and the last thing I want is for anyone to feel shamed or annoyed with themselves. Remember, we can begin doing things differently at any stage, and thanks to neuroplasticity, we can build more helpful neural pathways at any age.

GETTING STUCK IN AN EMOTION

Where possible, we need to be really mindful of listening to and validating these children. Empathic children feel a lot. If we don't experience the world this way, it can be easy to dismiss their feelings or try to move them on from a feeling. We don't want to see them sad or taking on worries that we feel are unnecessary. But when we try to move them on, or we don't allow them the space to process their emotional experience, they can get stuck. Once stuck, it is hard to get unstuck. To illustrate this, let's have a look at Katy's story.

> *Katy is a six-year-old who is feeling sad. Her best friend, Jennifer, sat beside another girl at lunchtime, and they didn't ask Katy to join in. Katy spent the rest of the day after school lying on the couch with a pain in her tummy. She refused to go swimming, saying that she felt too sad and that she didn't feel well. Her parents are both very practical, so this felt completely over the top to them. It was the fifth time this year Katy had come home from school acting this way over seemingly minor things. Her parents decided they would sit her down and help her begin to cope with this.*
>
> *'Katy, we know you are upset, love, but this is too*

much. All friendships change when you are growing up – that's life. You will probably be friends again later this week, so please try not to worry about it. We can't have you coming home from school and not going swimming anymore. No one else in your class acts this way, Katy, so it's time to grow up a little bit.'

'You don't understand! I don't want to talk to you. Go away!' Katy then runs to her room and slams the door.

While Katy's parents' intentions are good here, unfortunately, they may have inadvertently made her feel more alone. She has gone to her room feeling confused and angry with herself for her explosive outburst. She also feels confused and ashamed about her own reactions about Jennifer. She wonders why she is like this. Why does she care so much? What is wrong with her? She feels heavy and down, like a little light has turned off inside. Her emotions are stuck. She hasn't been able to let them out or process her feelings with her parents' help so her deep-processing mind is trying to make sense of it all. It is coming up with all sorts of explanations for her feelings. Her mind begins an anxious loop, thinking and processing, stuck in a cycle that is hard to make sense of.

'Looping' or feeling stuck often happens when we feel like our emotions don't make sense. I see this with the sensitive children I work with frequently, and this loop is often just part of their deep-processing brain. Being able to reflect on situations like this is a fantastic ability, but it can be a challenge too. If something happens and they feel sad, these children tend to loop back over it for days while they try and integrate it in their nervous system and make sense of their story. It can require some more 'digging deep' from us as we try to step into their mind and be patient and understanding, riding the wave of emotion with them and allowing space for it to be felt.

One thing that can make looping more challenging to get out of is if we ourselves had our emotions dismissed growing up. Again, this is not to blame anyone's parents – we just didn't have the same awareness around emotions as we do now. But if an emotion has been dismissed, there is a deep sense of confusion, and it can feel hard to move on because the big open feeling hasn't been taken care of. I have to work really hard on this. I can get stuck quite easily and stuck in a mood. If I have an argument with my husband and then we 'move on', it always takes me three times longer to let it go. One reason for this is that deep-feeling nervous system of mine has experienced the emotion so strongly that it takes time to lift. The other is because if the emotion hasn't been really seen and understood, then it takes far longer to be processed.

Let's go back to Katy to see what I mean.

> *'Katy, love, it's understandable you feel sad today. We know how much you care about Jennifer, and that must have really hurt you. I am sure you felt left out and disappointed they didn't ask you to sit with them. It can be so painful when we feel disconnected from our friends and we feel sad.'*

'Oh. I just feel so sad. I never want to go to school again. I wish I wasn't like this – why do I care so much?'

'I know, love. I get it. What happened today really hurt, and it can feel so hard to pick ourselves up from that. I remember something similar happened to me when I was your age and I felt sad too. And do you know what? You care so much because you are so kind. Your big heart is what makes you special. It just sucks sometimes that with that big heart come feelings that feel sore sometimes.'

'Yeah, okay – it's just so hard.'

Katy's parents sit with her while she cries. Notice the difference in this interaction. Katy's parents are not trying to fix it: they are just being with the emotion. This is the most powerful parenting tool you will ever have. Learning to be with painful feelings, without trying to fix them, is so connecting for our relationships – especially for our empaths. We need to understand that we can't talk them out of their feelings. The only way their emotions move is by giving them the space to be felt. It is only then that we can begin thinking of ideas that may help.

Katy's parents could begin brainstorming some ideas with Katy for when she goes into school the next day. Could she bring in a colouring book to share with Jennifer and the other girl at lunch as a way over to their table? They could help Katy practise taking a 360-degree view of the situation, questioning what might have been happening for Jennifer. Maybe Jennifer didn't notice Katy was sad and was just enjoying eating food with a new friend. We want to teach them how to take a compassionate approach.

Rather than saying, 'Oh, that was mean – Jennifer is not nice,' we want them to learn how to put themselves in another person's shoes and be open to another perspective.

Last year I was in a playground with my son. Two little boys, around age seven and eight, were having great fun going up and down the slides. They were so immersed in their play that they didn't see my eldest behind them. My son was running towards me in delight, so proud of himself for being brave enough to go down the slide. His big smile quickly vanished when one of the boys knocked him over. His little face crumpled into tears from the fright. The older boy shouted sorry behind him, and he rushed back to re-engage in his play.

How we respond to situations like this can really shape our children's world view. Again, don't be hard on yourself if you would be the person quick to jump in and say, 'That boy is so careless! He shouldn't have done that. Some people just don't care about others and are rude!' If this is your usual response, you most definitely have a point sometimes! Also, our world view is really shaped by our experiences. So if we grew up hearing this, or have spent our life so far feeling walked over and taken advantage of, then it makes sense our reactions would sound like this.

Ideally, though, we want to help our children to realise that *most* people mean well. Most people's intentions are kind. So while it is normal for our fight/flight/freeze/fawn to get activated and to feel angry or frustrated with others initially, we might then be able to step back and take the more compassionate perspective. That might sound like: 'Oh no, love, you got a big fright. I am so sorry. You were so happy running over to me and then that older boy knocked you down. He was so excited to get back up the slide that he didn't see you. I hope you are okay.'

It's not that we dismiss their emotions or try and 'be positive' in a forced way about the situation. We want to see their emotion, make it feel understood and minded. And at the same time, we want to model the compassionate perspective about other people. This is particularly important for our empaths. They are really special little souls, and if we nurture this quality in a gentle way, their tender hearts feel soothed. Life can feel easier when we learn most people are just trying to do their best, when we see behaviour as the outer layer and are open and curious enough to see what's underneath. This helps our children begin to mentalise, which is the fantastic skill of being able to put themselves in someone else's shoes.

PROTECTING THEIR HEARTS

Our empaths need to be guided carefully as they grow. While it is a fantastic thing to be able to empathise with other people, we need to help protect their big hearts. We need to be mindful of this at home where possible. These children are highly attuned to our emotions. Like little sponges, they soak in the energy and the moods around them. Given that we are the most important thing in the world to them, it makes sense they are even more aware of how we are.

This doesn't mean they should never see us cry or feel angry or that we should have to hide any emotion! It is actually really helpful for our empaths to see us experience a wide range of emotions. These deeply feeling children are experiencing emotions all the time. So if we model this as being completely normal, along with how to mind ourselves, it is a huge gift to them. They will grow up believing that their feelings are nothing to be ashamed of. It will be easier for them to process them and help them move on. We just need to be mindful of talking about emotional topics around them that are not necessarily age appropriate. Examples might be discussing problems in our romantic relationships, negative self-talk or frustrations we have with family and so on. No parent does this on purpose, but sometimes our children become more like a friend to us. This is not to say we shouldn't be friends with our children – it is a beautiful thing to have a close relationship with them. We just need to be careful that we are not relying on them to meet our needs, the way we might in our own relationships with adults.

Sometimes we might tell our children about arguments we are having with each other. We might say things like: 'Your dad/mom wasn't very nice to me earlier. I am so sad. Thankfully I have you to talk to – you are always so kind to me.' We have to be really careful if we find ourselves saying things like this. This isn't meant to shame or scare anyone; we all say things like this from time to time. It's just that these little empaths begin to take our feelings on as if they are their own. They can move into 'fixer' mode far too early and take on an adult role where they begin minding us. This can feel really comforting to the parent who has this deep connection with their child. But we might not notice the impact this has on our children.

Internally, they might be feeling worried and unsure. They are so highly emotionally attuned that they recognise they need to help us feel better. If we remember a child's attachment relationship is the most important thing in their world, we know that any threat to this feels scary. So they might work extra hard to please us, to comfort us, to repair our relationships. Please do not be hard on yourself if you have fallen into this dynamic with your child. Knowledge is power, and it's difficult to know how to navigate parenting sometimes – especially with our own childhood wounding and our wonderful and messy life histories.

I was quite taken aback at my own reflections on this recently. I was watching a family movie with my son. I received a message on my phone with some bad news. I started to cry, and my son asked me what was wrong. I explained I was sad about some news I'd just got and that I wasn't upset with him. He said, 'Oh no. I am so sorry, Mommy. I love you so much,' and came over to give me a hug. We sat there for a moment while he rubbed my head. 'You will be okay, Mommy, I am here.'

This interaction was really interesting to me because I could understand so deeply how easy it could be to lean on these little people for support. Without meaning to, we might begin talking to them about our problems and looking for their advice as they get older. Again, there is nothing wrong with having close relationships – it is such a lovely thing. We just need to be cautious that we do not forget they are *children* who need our support, comfort and guidance, and not the other way around. We have to be careful that we don't confuse their emotional intuition for wisdom and maturity. We need to let them be kids as long as we can. Life is tough on our empaths, and the illusion of safety in the world sadly doesn't last all that long. So wherever we can, we need to protect them from taking on too much. It might be helpful to reflect here on the things that we say to them and notice if we lean on them for support. Do we worry them about our work stress, financial concerns, relationship problems, mental health challenges and so on? Again, we're not giving out to ourselves for this, just redirecting our support-seeking towards other adults in our life.

To be clear, it doesn't mean we are not open with our children. It's just that we do it in a developmentally appropriate way, and we remember that it's our job to mind them, not the other way around. So we can be open about our emotions, worries and so on but remind them that we are the adult and that they have nothing to worry about. We might say something like: 'I am just a bit sad and worried, love. I see you are upset for me too, and thank you so much for caring. You have the biggest heart and I love you so much. I will be okay, and I have lots of people helping me with this.' We don't want to shield them or have secret conversations that they are aware of, making them wonder what is going on. If this happens, they tend to come up with all sorts of hypotheses and may feel anxious and unsure. So where possible, we can be transparent while remembering to reassure them that, even if we are struggling, we have support and we will be okay.

Helping our empaths feel included

The empath usually feels older than their years. They might find it frustrating not to be included in important conversations. They might start to feel left out if we are saying things like: 'This is an adult conversation – it's not for your ears'. We can try to be a little gentler in how we communicate this to these kids, remembering they often feel like an adult in their head and want to deeply connect with us, so hearing this might feel like a rejection to them. They might start to feel like we don't understand them or want to connect with them the way they do with us. Instead, we might say, 'We hear how much you want to be involved, love. Thank you, your thoughts and ideas are always so important to us. We are discussing something that only needs our thinking heads right now, but we promise if there's anything important, we will fill you in.'

You could come up with a little plan to help them feel included later on by saying something like: 'Thank you for being so patient earlier and letting us finish our conversation. Now we do actually need your help with something! We need to discuss the plan after school on Friday. We have an option of going to Grandad's house or going over to play in Charlie's. What would you prefer, love?'

That might sound a bit simplistic, but these children really thrive when they are given a sense of involvement. They love feeling like they are part of the decision-making, and it helps foster their skills in this area. It also helps them feel included and important. Ideally, we want to be the first people who make them feel valued and that someone is excited to hear what they have to say. Psychologists call this to 'delight' in our children. We show them clearly with both verbal and non-verbal cues just how much we love them. This can be something simple you add into your day, like allowing your smile to really light up your face when you see them. It's a small practice that has a dramatic influence on our relationships. Think about how you greet your partner, if you have one, or your friends, your family members, your own parents. How do they greet you? Is there a difference in how you feel being greeted by a friend and by someone you don't know very well? Think about that person in your life who, when they greet you, their smile reaches every part of their eyes, and you know just how happy they are to see you.

Because our empaths pick up on our moods and emotions so quickly, we have to work extra hard on our tone of voice and facial expression when we see them. That may sound exhausting, and it doesn't mean to force positivity when that doesn't reflect our feelings, but we might just stay mindful of it, reminding ourselves how making them feel so loved will likely pour warmth into their open energy zones. So many of us when we are stressed are a little curt in our responses, or we might be less aware of our verbal and non-verbal cues. But if we can really 'delight' in them when we see them, like we would with someone we love and haven't seen in a while, they feel loved and cared for. Big hugs and kisses when we can and telling them how much we love them mean so much. We might think they know this, but it's always good to be intentional in how we say it and to show it in our words and in our actions. Saying it and hoping they know we mean it isn't always enough. They need to really *feel* our love for them. A simple thing like learning to delight in them is a brilliant step towards this.

Staying open to learning from our empaths

We could all learn a lot if we really listened to the innocence of children and their thoughts and views of the world. Our empathic children lead with their hearts, so they might begin to challenge us when they hear our judgements about people or situations.

> *Andrew is an eleven-year-old who overheard his parents talking about someone in his class. They were talking about his race and socioeconomic status and that he was 'different'. Andrew remembers feeling confused. He had noticed his friend looked and spoke differently to him, but he hadn't viewed him as different before. Andrew could pick up on the tone his parents used and the hint of disapproval in their voices. He questioned what they meant as that deep-processing brain of his tried to fit the missing pieces of the puzzle together. He now saw his friend through a different lens. For the first time in his life, he realised he felt disappointed in his parents. He felt strongly that just because someone lived in and through different circumstances, it didn't make them less than. He challenged his parents on this, but they dismissed the topic and moved on.*

My biggest piece of advice with these children is to really listen to what they have to say. It's not our fault, but sadly we have all internalised many preconceived ideas and judgements about the 'other' that have been conditioned since we were children. It means we need to be open to the fact that we have a lot to unlearn, and no better person to show us that than a sensitive child growing up. If we take the time to hear them and watch the world through their eyes, we can allow some of our own guards to drop. There is a freedom in knowing there is so much we don't know! The day we think we have nothing to learn is the day we know we need to question ourselves. Life as we know it is constantly changing, and we can model our willingness to work on our blind spots without blame and shame.

Boundaries

A very important skill empaths need to learn is how to be boundaried with their energy. I have to work extremely hard at this myself, and I still don't get it right all the time. So we need to be really proactive in helping our children with this. The world we live in is a beautiful yet painful one. We are all aware of heartbreaking sadness, grief and loss every day. With constant access to the news and media, we are even more aware now of the challenges and horrifying circumstances our fellow humans are going through. We also see the devastating impact climate change is having on our planet, and we are exposed to how our actions are contributing to this. This is a good thing in many ways, as it spurs so many of us to take action. It helps us care about the environment and each other, reminding us that we are part of something bigger. If we open our minds and our hearts, we can see how incredibly powerful the collective is.

The difficulty here is that we can also easily fall into hopelessness. Those with big hearts can feel swallowed up by pain sometimes. I know that might sound extreme, but that is genuinely how it feels. If we are not careful with how much we care, we can collapse into despair. This happens to me sometimes when I forget to mind myself or pop on my protective cloak. It doesn't mean I look away completely, but I have learned how to channel my sadness into action.

I know that feeling overcome by sadness and grief about the unjustness in the world is not going to help anyone, least of all myself. So what I teach the children I work with, and always remind myself, is to channel our empathy into compassion. If we don't take steps to mind ourselves with this, it can result in a very sore heart, as life can feel overwhelming. Moving from empathy to compassion means moving from feeling the emotion to being able to respond with small actions while we take the focus back off ourselves. This helps us to create meaning around experiences and know how to help. One of the most helpful things we can do as parents of these children is to become passionate about their passions, so if your child cares deeply about something, sit down and formulate a plan together about something you can do. Is there a local charity you can volunteer with? Is there a climate change advocacy group for families you could join? Could they organise a plastic clean-up on the beach or a rubbish clean-up in the park? Let's say, for example, your child has seen a TV programme about animals being mistreated and they have been deeply impacted by this. They are devastated there is such cruelty in the world. This could be a great opportunity to help them process their pain in a compassionate way. Perhaps there is an animal shelter nearby that you could volunteer with, or you could sit down together and write letters to local officials expressing your concerns.

I can't stress this enough: teaching our children how to take care of their big hearts and move towards compassion will help hugely with protecting their empathy. I often reflect on this in my job. While being a psychologist probably seems like a natural move for an empath, it could be a very challenging one if I didn't know how to protect myself. I care so deeply about the people I work with and mirror their suffering and pain closely sometimes. If I am under-resourced, this can get tricky, as I can feel overcome by the sadness they are experiencing and feel so heartbroken for the circumstances they are in. Every day, I have to actively practise allowing myself to feel their pain and then channel this pain into compassion and helping. Learning how to pop on a protective cloak just means knowing when I need to physically shift my energy. This can help us all when we begin to sink into feeling down – learning how to say, 'Hey! You're okay – I've got you! Up you get,' and physically shift our energy.

Believe them and their emotions

Trusting our children when they feel sad about something is very powerful. Try to remain open and willing to listen, even when it sounds a little bit much. A child who cries about standing on a snail by accident, while it might seem extreme, is likely feeling a huge range of emotions. The first step to helping them is to just acknowledge their feelings. Dive into their world with a curious mind as you hear the impact this has had on them. Try to remember that it's only when they feel understood that we can help them move through it. We won't always be able to fix things or cheer them up, but that's okay. Their inner ability to soothe will come in time.

Let's have a look at Izzy's story.

> *Izzy is a five-year-old with lots of big feelings and a very big heart. Her family are worried about her, as they notice she tends to take on the emotions of others. When she's around people who are happy and excited, she seems full of life and at ease in herself. When she is around people who are sad or worried, she seems stressed and down. She can't watch the same TV shows or movies as her siblings because that big heart of hers hurts for anyone who is sad or in pain. She finds unfairness difficult to understand and asks lots of questions about the world and about people who are suffering. Her parents notice she is becoming more anxious the more she is exposed to the world. They know they can't shield her from this but also worry about the toll these emotions are having on her.*
>
> *Not only is she connecting with the emotions of others, but she is also physically feeling them too. This is an incredible gift, as it helps her relate to and understand others around her. The difficulty is that Izzy is still so young, and she has not learned how to protect herself with this. It will take time for her to learn how to separate her feelings from someone else's and that she is not responsible for fixing*

someone else's mood. Izzy's parents feel understandably stressed about this. They also feel under pressure not to feel sad or show their emotions at home.

Izzy's parents are reminded that it's okay to show their feelings. One of the best ways Izzy will learn how to manage all of this for herself is by watching how they mind themselves when they feel their emotions too. They begin to teach Izzy to notice that her big heart tends to take on the emotions of others at times. They help her to be curious around this and have a little 'self-soothe pack' for when she notices she feels overwhelmed.

For example, when Izzy comes home from school feeling sad that Lisa was left out of a game, they help her practise a safe-space bubble. They acknowledge it must have been hard to see Lisa upset and remind her that it's lovely that she cares so much about her friends. They say, 'I notice the sadness is really heavy in your heart. I wonder could we spend some time in your bubble?' They then make a big imaginary bubble around Izzy where the sadness waits outside for a few moments. This bubble contains all of the memories or stories that make her smile. Her parents go into this imaginary bubble too, joining in with colouring or breathing exercises to help her feel at ease while she is having some space from sadness. They are slowly teaching her how to create a little distance from painful feelings and to protect herself.

Another important step is helping Izzy step into her compassionate self. They empower her to plan what she *will do to help Lisa, as she cares so much about her. Izzy decides she will draw a little picture for Lisa with a heart on it and get some help from her parents to write a note saying she loves her and thanking her for being her special friend. Izzy also decides she is going to make sure Lisa is involved in any game she is playing tomorrow. Izzy feels much better now that she has a plan to help her friend.*

You might sit down with your own child and think about what helps them, then design your own self-soothe kit for when they feel down or need some comforting. Help them learn how to check in with themselves and ask themselves these three questions:

- How am I feeling in my head and body? 'Oh, I feel sad because Jane's mom was mean to her and I can see she is upset. I feel that heavy feeling in my chest.'
- What do I need right now? 'To remind myself it's okay to feel sad and give myself a hug.'
- What can I do? 'I will give Jane a hug and tell her I am here for her.'

The following guide might continue to help you as you raise your little empath.

- Practise becoming aware of your own moods, remembering that, unfortunately for us, our moods tend to impact these children more than their less-sensitive peers.

- Remind yourself you don't have to fake it! If we are feeling low or having a bad day, that's okay. The most important piece here is that we express our feelings openly.
- Model treating yourself with kindness and compassion, remembering children learn most not from our words, but from what we do.
- Model treating others with empathy and compassion, remembering we have a unique ability to nurture this incredible gift in our children.
- Nurture their big hearts. Help them to see what a beautiful trait they have. Help them to see how special it is to feel so deeply and to care so much. Remind them how lucky you feel to have them in your life.
- Nurture a sense of agency. Foster their interests and passions. Allow them to believe they have a sense of control in the world. They may not be able to fix everything, but we can teach them that every little helps.
- Finally … be kind to yourself! You can only do your best, so try not to put yourself under pressure, and remember that these kids will continue to surprise you as they grow.

CHAPTER 7

Criticism and 'being good'

Criticism is complex and can feel painful for any of us. This pain runs particularly deep for the sensitive child because they are so in tune with their emotions and other people's perceptions of them. As their nervous system is so sensitive to subtle stimuli, they often pick up on it immediately if someone feels negatively towards them. Thanks to their deep-processing brains, they also may ruminate on times when they felt criticised, which can amplify its impact.

They tend to be quite conscientious (not always, I know!) in the way they conduct themselves and in everything they apply themselves to. Being so aware of other people's thoughts and feelings often makes sensitive children want to 'be good'. This can stem from a really genuine place, as we see the beauty of their empathy beginning to shine through. They care about us and about their teachers, peers and significant others, so they try to meet our expectations, and when they inevitably and humanly do something 'wrong', the feedback can feel particularly hurtful to a big heart that yearns to be loved and accepted.

Criticism and the sensitive child

You most likely have noticed that criticism, whether in terms of how they are doing something like playing a sport or perceived negative feedback about their behaviour, seems to be quite painful for your child. This can be a challenge to navigate, as parents often say that what their child is perceiving as criticism is meant as constructive feedback. Parents worry that maybe their child will never be able to accept criticism and that life will be much more challenging as a result. Try and remain hopeful with this if you can, and know that we have enormous potential to help them learn how to navigate these complex emotions.

Something we can be really mindful of with sensitive children is trying our best not to shame them. A disappointed glance from us, or vocalising our disapproval of a sensitive child's behaviour, sets off a little alarm in their threat response, as they are so attuned to subtle shifts in our responses. If we don't help them process the situation but continue to be disappointed in them or disapproving, they often internalise this, leading to feelings of shame and impacting their sense of self-worth. This is complicated, as parents understandably get a fright sometimes if their child has done something inappropriate. The parents are trying their best and can't help questioning their child or criticising their behaviour in front of other parents, teachers, peers and so on. We need to be cautious in doing this if possible. Think about your own experiences of being criticised. Were you ever publicly reprimanded by your own parent, teacher or peer? It is often particularly painful if we have experienced this from significant caregivers, as it can break trust and weaken our connection with them if a repair doesn't happen. It can make our children more socially anxious, or they may try harder to please others and fit in – anything to avoid the humiliation of being shamed again.

These are the children who feel it deep in their bones if they are being left out or made fun of. I have had a lot of younger clients who had sadly stopped playing sports or joining in activities because they were sensitive to rejection and disappointment from team members. These kids can be so hard on themselves when they make a mistake and when someone corrects their behaviour. This is because they try so hard to do well and want nothing more than to feel accepted by peers or other important people in their life. So feeling like they have let people down or disappointed others in some way can shake them to their core. Unfortunately, a huge part of this has often been the tone in which feedback is delivered. These children can be very sensitive to words that are delivered in harsh or accusing tones – 'Ah, come on, how did you mess that up?' 'Uh, seriously? If you had just kicked the ball!' 'Wake up, are you even on the pitch?' 'Wakey, wakey – anyone online in that brain of yours today?' 'Are you even listening to my instructions?' Even if some of this feedback is meant in a more light-hearted manner, this type of 'banter' can feel like a painful personal attack to a child with a deep-feeling heart. Harshness is perceived as mean and hurts them on a deeper level. It can really knock their confidence and create a sense of feeling different and loneliness. They may begin to feel like they shouldn't bother trying or like they will never truly fit in. This drives some children to try extra hard to please and 'be perfect' and will drive others to shut down and avoid. The emotion centres in their brain can feel like they're on fire and they want to run away and hide, or they might lash out in anger. That deep-processing brain tends to ruminate on the situation, and they find themselves feeling very low and sad, internalising their emotions and beating themselves up for being 'stupid' or 'not good enough'. Or they externalise their emotions by letting it out with attacking energy – you might hear things like: 'You did it wrong!', 'It's your fault I can't do it', or 'I hate football anyway'.

One of the best ways we can help them with this is by being mindful of our tone and how we deliver feedback to them, and also by helping them to understand this in themselves. We might explain to them that the reason criticism feels so painful is because those big hearts of theirs care so much. 'I get it, pet. I am so sorry you feel upset. I completely understand how those words hurt.' We can explain how understandable it is to feel bad about themselves or feel angry in response to this. We can help them see that, while they might not have mastered a certain skill just yet, that does not mean they will never get there. They might need a lot of our support and encouragement to stick with something they are finding challenging – to learn to just take it step by step and know that we will be there to guide them through it. We can help them understand that none of us is perfect at everything, and our confidence grows from our mistakes and learning what to do the next time.

We can also validate their experience by telling them a similar story about when we were growing up. 'Two of my team members used to say things that felt mean to me too. I came to realise this was just the way they talked, and they didn't mean to insult me personally. It still always hurt a little when they did it, but it helped knowing it wasn't personal.' You might teach them something to say when it happens again – for example, 'Hey, go easy! I am doing my best.' If it continues, we can guide them in speaking to their teacher, coach or peer by saying, 'I really am doing my best. When you speak to me like that, I feel upset and embarrassed. Do you mind not speaking to me like that anymore?' And we can also praise them for their efforts where we can. Sometimes we believe our children know we are proud of them, and in the busyness of everyday we forget to say it! When we say it, and then say it again and again, our sensitive children can feel this warmth and love on a cellular level, and it helps their confidence and sense of self-worth to grow.

Something I struggle with is not being too critical about my children's behaviour while they have such little impulse control. It's not easy with two mischievous boys who find it hilarious to turn our house upside down! Understanding the why behind their behaviour can be so helpful for us and for them. They often do things without thinking and love to test our limits, which is a developmentally expected part of being a child. If we think back to a more old-school parenting approach, we might have been led to believe our children are doing something 'on purpose' and/

or are intentionally trying to 'be bold' at these times. I have worked with some wonderful parents who feel so activated when their child behaves this way and unconsciously respond punitively, as the behaviour would never have been accepted from them by their own parents.

> *Lilly is a three-year-old whose grandparent just bought her a beautiful book all about space and the stars. She is sitting at the table one morning reading her book and feeling giddy inside. She decides it would be funny to rip a few pages of her book and throw them on the floor. Her parents feel so angry with her and demand to know how she could be so careless. How could she have such little respect for her things? 'You are bold, Lilly. Gran will be so disappointed when we tell her what you have done. No more presents for you – we are disgusted that you did that.'*

You may read that and feel, ouch, poor Lilly, and/or relate on some level with Lilly's parents. It is easy to say, 'I would never speak to my child that way', but the reality is, it is a very human response to feel annoyed, and much of parenting is our own inner-child wounds becoming activated too. We often react and respond from our emotional brain and it's only afterwards that we reflect and think, 'Hmm, maybe that was a bit harsh'. And if our behaviour was responded to in a punitive manner when we were small and we haven't processed this or reflected on the impact of it within ourselves, it makes sense this pattern is recreated and becomes our default response. And sometimes we are already feeling stressed with managing so many demands, and 'one more thing' just pushes us out of our window of tolerance. So please be kind to yourselves, as always, if reading this feels familiar.

What could be useful to Lilly here would be helping her understand that we all do things sometimes without thinking. Her brain is still developing, and she might act on impulse or urges! We might explore what was going through her mind when she tore the book. 'You felt giddy today and ripped your book without thinking. It's hard to understand why we do things sometimes, I know! I am sorry for shouting, Lilly. I got a fright when I saw you do that. I know you didn't mean it and it's not your fault.' We might then explain why it's important to mind our things, gently explaining how thoughtful it was of Gran to buy the book because she loves Lilly, and this incident is a good opportunity to practise feeling grateful for having books and having someone who cares for us in this way.

Sometimes we believe we need to be harsh and punitive to teach our children a lesson. We may believe that is the only way they will really listen to us and learn from their mistakes. While it is true that shaming them about their behaviour will make it less likely they will do it again, it also creates more anxiety and internal unease. Their deep-processing brains latch on to every time we shame them about their behaviour, and it becomes part of the story they tell themselves about who they are. Please don't worry too much if you have been doing this! We can help our children with this at any stage, and it could be a really helpful conversation to begin. If you have been harsher and more punitive in the past, you might sit down with them and say, 'I know I was pretty hard on you before, love, and I know you felt sad and annoyed with yourself (and/or me!). I'm sorry for doing that. Sometimes I get stressed, and I say things quickly that I don't mean. It's hard growing up, and I remember lots of times I did things that I regretted afterwards too! None of us are perfect.' This kind of repair is something we can always work on. Never underestimate the power of this and of reconnecting with them after a period of disconnection.

The reason it is so important to be mindful of not shaming them about their behaviour is because they are most likely already doing it. They probably already hold themselves to high standards and try to be careful in how they conduct themselves. So if they do or say something wrong, they might feel angry towards themselves. The way they begin talking to themselves during these times becomes their own internal voice as they grow. This is something we have to be mindful of as parents because many of us sensitive souls have an internal critic that is loud and harsh. We can help counteract this as their caregivers by stepping into a wise, compassionate adult role that guides them with this. Rather than doubling up on their own critical voice, we model speaking kindly to them. We help them view their behaviour with gentle curiosity rather than a punitive voice. We have such an important role here in helping to shape their future sense of self-worth and confidence.

You might be thinking, 'Aoife, you're making this sound a lot easier than it is.' Believe me, I know! Recently I said these words to my three-year-old: 'You're so mean – I can't believe you did that! You're mean!' I get it, it's so hard sometimes and parenting can feel so challenging. This is especially true when we are exhausted, and we just don't have it in the tank. Sometimes I reach the end of the day and feel like I have run a marathon. I am emotionally and physically drained and one more stress just feels too much. So I write this with the utmost compassion and understanding for you all. Remember, you can only do your best. You can work hard on repair too when, like me, you act in ways that are not so helpful. You can model being compassionate to yourself by giving yourself a break and not beating yourself up. And you can apologise to your child. For me, this sounded like: 'I am so sorry for calling you mean, love. I know you are just tired, and you didn't mean to hit your brother. I am tired too, and I got a fright when I saw him crying. Hitting really hurts people – it's not okay to hit, and I am just trying to help you know how to be gentle. Can you tell me next time you're frustrated with him so I can help you before the hits happen?'

MOVING ON FROM FEELING STUCK WHEN CRITICISED

Another thing you may have noticed is how hard it is for some of our children to move on if they have felt criticised. They might ask, 'Why were you mean to me?' or 'Why did you give out to me?' again and again as their mind tries to piece the puzzle together. In these moments it can be helpful for us to remember that their deep-processing brain is trying to make sense of their emotions. In chapter six, I mentioned how they often loop back to the difficult situation or seem to 'hold a grudge' against the person they felt criticised by. This can be hard to manage, and you may feel like saying, 'Aw, come on! Move on!'

However, I would encourage you to do the opposite of telling them to move on. If you have anything in the tank, these are the moments we need to dig deep, reminding ourselves that they are a little stuck in the depths of their feelings and that being a kind and caring presence will slowly help soften their emotions. One of the most frustrating things I find about myself is how deeply tangled I can become if I feel hurt by someone's words or actions. I often feel like I am stuck in a web that I want to get out of, yet I am too entwined. When we are left to deal with our emotions alone, or when they are minimised or dismissed, this often leaves them with nowhere to go. The result of this is that, over time, we tend to internalise our emotions and don't learn how to help ourselves become 'unstuck'.

Something that always helps me with myself, my children and the children I work with is to remember to give them time when this happens. How much time they need is individual to each child, but with our validation, acceptance and support their emotions will begin to soften over time.

> *Olivia is nine, and she has a close friend in school called Ciara. Ciara confided in Olivia one day, telling her she had bought her first-ever bra, but she didn't want any of the girls in the class to know. When Ciara was off sick from school the following week, some of the other girls were talking about her at lunchtime. Farah said, 'Girls, I think I saw Ciara is wearing a bra under her clothes! She*

definitely is but she is too embarrassed to tell anyone.' Olivia *impulsively answered, wanting to fit in with the pack, 'She told me! But please don't tell her I told you.' Farah smiled knowingly. 'Oh, we won't.'*

I am sure you can guess how the rest of this story ends. Ciara is confronted about her new bra in front of the class when she comes back, and when she tries to deny it, Farah is quick to inform her that Olivia confirmed it. Time slows down for Olivia as she registers the disappointment and hurt on Ciara's face. Ciara just quietly delivers feedback to Olivia, saying, 'Thanks a lot. I know who I will never trust again anyway.' Olivia realises she has betrayed her friend's trust, and rather than feeling guilty about her actions, she feels the powerful force of shame. 'I am a horrible person – how could I do that to my friend?'

We may not understand why the criticism or feedback hurt so much – it might feel 'childish' or insignificant to us – but for these big-hearted, big-feeling children it most likely feels all-encompassing. Shame is one of the most painful emotions any of us (highly sensitive or not) can experience. Our brain and nervous system registers shame in the same way it registers strong physical pain. When we notice our children have gone into a shame spiral, we should try to validate their emotional experience, without trying to fix it or push it away. We should remind ourselves that shame dies when stories are told in safe places. So if we can provide a kind and gentle listening ear, their emotions might process and move more quickly. We need to be proactive with our children when they feel ashamed. We need to remember that it's in the retelling of stories where we make meaning about our behaviour or other people's behaviour towards us. This is what helps shame and feeling criticised hurt less. We might work on being particularly vulnerable with our kids and telling them about times in the past when we felt the same. We want them to know that we all make mistakes, none of us are perfect, and it's what we learn and what we do after we make mistakes that matters.

HELPING THEM FIND THEIR VOICE

It is good to practise teaching children to say, 'Please don't talk to me like that', to use 'I' statements like 'I feel sad when you tell me I can't play' rather than saying 'You're mean', and when to walk away from situations they feel uncomfortable in. My three-year-old recently said to me, 'Mommy, you're speaking loudly and it doesn't sound like you are being very kind' when he overheard a heated discussion I was having with my own mom! They really are little sponges. We can reinforce this ability in them by thanking them for saying no and for letting us know how they feel, even if it is difficult for us to hear. We might say, 'Thank you for pointing out that I wasn't speaking kindly. I appreciate your letting me know. I will work on this.' When we remain open to hearing this feedback, it helps them develop their own skills for setting boundaries in their friendships and in their relationships with teachers and other significant people in their life. They begin to learn that their relationships with us remain steady, even when they want to voice something that we may not agree with.

Our children often re-enact these situations in their play. At the moment, we are playing a lot of 'good guys and baddies', where my son plays out little scenarios of feeling left out or trying to make sense of challenging situations. He is resolving it through 'tying up the baddies' in his play and letting his frustration out. It is fascinating how their little minds process their feelings. Allowing them the space to do this and getting involved in their play too can be hugely beneficial for this. Try not to worry about this type of play if you can. Of course we might worry about more 'aggressive' play and that it will transfer into their relationships. But play is a beautiful way that our children process their little hurts. And this kind of play can be particularly helpful for our conscientious children who try to 'do the right thing'. Having the freedom to explore this other 'powerful' side of them can be so freeing. My advice is to join them in it if you can and have fun! If this type of behaviour begins to occur in their relationships outside of play, then this could indicate that they need some support. They might have experienced something painful, and it is manifesting in more attacking energy.

Many of us worry about how to teach them to stick up for themselves and hate the thought of them struggling to find their voice with peers. We need to try and soothe ourselves here and remember that modelling this at home and watching how we hold boundaries with others is powerful. So too is the safe space we create at home where they can talk to us about peer dynamics they are struggling with. And we need to give ourselves permission to step back sometimes, remembering that often how we learn this is from our mistakes and sadly it's often the hard way that builds resilience to this. The one thing we can do is to remain that safe space and listening ear. Never underestimate how incredibly healing and powerful this is. Although its success might not be something we can measure immediately, you are helping wire your child's brain to be more compassionate and understanding towards themselves in the future. This helps protect their mental health and is one of the biggest gifts you can give them.

The sensitive child and being good

Sometimes our sensitive children find criticism so painful that they work extra hard to ensure they don't have to feel that way. We might remember from previous chapters that while we develop these 'protectors' to help us feel safe, over time they create more anxiety and unease. Our child may become fixated with being 'good' so that they don't make a mistake and don't have to feel the discomfort of feeling ashamed, rejected or dismissed.

If your child gets really worried about doing the right thing or feeling like they have disappointed you, know that this is quite common, and it doesn't mean you have caused this stress or anxiety. They pick up so much from the world around them, from peers, school, television. They also tend to internalise our emotions so it's important to try not to shame them for their behaviour, as discussed above. We want to be careful about saying things like 'You make me so sad when you don't ...' or sending them the message that they are responsible for our feelings.

This can be particularly hard when they are younger, and their brains are still in the early stages of development. They might feel stressed inside and then use their body to try and regulate their overwhelmed nervous system. This means their emotions are often expressed physically in the form of hitting, kicking, throwing and so on. A trap I often fall into, along with many of the parents I work with, is misunderstanding my child's ability to articulate their emotions as the same thing as being able to control and regulate their emotions. We often expect more from our sensitive children as they are so emotionally in tune and articulate. We forget that they are still being driven mainly from their emotional brain with limited impulse control! We might think they understand why a behaviour isn't helpful and then feel confused and exasperated when they continue doing it when we tell them not to. They may have an intuitive sense that something like hitting isn't okay, but their little bodies are reacting from their emotional brain. They might begin to feel anxious about this unhelpful behaviour and become fixated on 'being good'. If this happens for your child, here is something you could say to them. 'I hear you saying you are a good girl – that's okay, love, I know! I love you so much and you're such a great person. It's normal to feel upset or angry sometimes. I shout too when I get stressed. Can you tell me a little more about what you are worried about?'

Because these sensitive souls are so attuned to our emotions, they naturally want to please us and be 'good'. As a result of this, they might push down their own needs as a way of staying connected with us. This is something we need to watch out for so that we can help them use their voice and learn how to say no or when they don't like something. This story about me as a child might be helpful.

When I was younger, my dad loved making us dinners he hoped we would enjoy. I watched him pottering away in the kitchen, and I could see early on how much thought and effort went into this. One of these dinners is a special pasta dish with sun-dried tomatoes. I love them now, but as a child I wasn't too keen on the taste of the sun-dried tomatoes. As a sensitive little soul, I was highly attuned to his emotions and how kind the intention was behind this dinner. My deep-processing brain used to come up with a little pros and cons list for telling him I didn't like the sun-dried tomatoes. Each time the cons outweighed the pros for me, as I worried I would hurt his feelings. I loved this time with him so much, and I worried that saying I didn't like the dish would somehow ruin it all. So I continued to eat the sun-dried tomato pasta even though I found the taste difficult.

How do we make sense of this behaviour through a psychological lens? One hypothesis is that I was afraid to say I didn't like it because I would be given out to. Or perhaps my dad would withdraw his care in some way. If that was the case, we can see how people-pleasing tendencies become activated. They become woven in tightly for sensitive children as they push down their own needs to stay connected to their caregivers. They realise early on that love and connectedness come from making others happy. And if they don't, the response is often critical, punitive or the subtle, but just as painful, feeling of being ignored.

There is another hypothesis here, and one that is often

misunderstood in sensitive children and adults. This is that some people are so highly aware of the emotions of others that they conduct their behaviour more carefully, as they consider all potential outcomes. So if a sensitive child sees another's intentions and thoughtfulness, pushing down their own needs might seem like the most natural outcome – not because there will be an unhelpful response, but because they care about the other person and want them to feel appreciated.

This is so important to understand in sensitive children. A child doesn't have the cognitive capacity to apply our adult critical-thinking skills to their behaviour. They don't know yet that they are not responsible for other people's feelings. So what starts out as an intrinsic motivation to help others can, over time, turn into the more complex psychological survival strategy of people-pleasing. We have enormous potential to help them with this. We can model saying no without negative consequences and check in with them about their behaviour. We need to be proactive around helping them to see it's okay to question our decisions, to disagree, to say no and that we still love them no matter what. We can tell them stories like this one to help them understand themselves. Stories are an incredibly powerful way to help them make meaning about how they interact in the world.

THE CHILD WHO APOLOGISES A LOT (AND THE ONE WHO DOESN'T!)

You may notice your child seems to apologise a lot and feel unsure about how to help them with this. Naturally empathic, they might feel impacted by someone else's emotions and say sorry even if they haven't done anything wrong. This is quite common with these children, and again it doesn't mean you have done anything wrong as a parent. Understanding this and being aware of it gives us a huge opportunity to help them.

As parents we want our children to feel okay, so if we hear them apologising for things they didn't do, we might immediately say, 'Don't be sorry – you did nothing wrong!' This is understandable – it is so hard seeing them struggle. But it is really helpful over time if, instead of rushing in to make them feel okay, we help them become curious about the need to apologise. We can do this by gently questioning their apology. 'I notice you are saying sorry again, love. I wonder what you are saying sorry for. Are you worried about something? You are so sensitive and caring about other people. It is a wonderful thing to have such a kind heart. I wonder if we could try being curious about the sorry next time it happens?' We can help them to practise 'pressing pause' and grounding themselves in the moment and beginning to notice their need to apologise. For example, helping them take a few deep breaths, gently swaying and releasing the tension from their body. Over time, we can help them learn to check in with themselves and others without immediately apologising. Modelling forgiveness for ourselves and others is one of the most helpful things we can teach children. We can show them that it's okay to make mistakes, and we can model self-compassion when we act or they act in ways that aren't so helpful, the main message being that we all make mistakes, and our behaviour does not define who we are.

I'm sure many of you are thinking, 'I wish my child would

apologise! I keep telling them to and they won't.' I hear you, and I know how activating this can be. I know how stressful it feels when our children appear 'rude' and might not say sorry and please or thank you. It is understandable that we worry about this, and many of us worry about our child's moral compass when we don't see them apologising. This is something I hear often from parents of sensitive children, especially those who are slow to warm. We might need to work on reframing this in our heads and remembering that their deep-processing brains are taking their time to figure out how they feel about something. So, for example, if a grandparent gives them a present and we watch our child hold it tentatively, examining it slowly before they respond, often our own stress response becomes activated, and we might push them to 'say thank you!' Or it might become activated for us when we see them do something and feel the need to remind them, 'That's not very nice – you should say sorry now'. Despite knowing how normal it is for children to, for example, take a child's toy without asking, push ahead of another child in the queue for the slide and so on, I still find I often reactively respond to my children this way. My own worry about the other adult feeling offended kicks into gear and I react from this place.

If, like me, you feel anxious about these things sometimes, remind yourself that children become intrinsically motivated to say sorry, please and thank you when they really mean it. And this naturally occurs from listening and watching how we respond. So try to model this for them as much as you can at home, and take the pressure off yourself in social situations, knowing they will all get there in their own way in time. While we can force them to say it, this unfortunately often has the opposite effect, and they only do it to please us or gain some kind of 'reward'. They become externally motivated. We can see here how people-pleasing tendencies may become activated too if they continue to feel like they are disappointing us. Remember, these children have big hearts and often internalise our emotions if they believe this is the case and may begin to please us from a fear of losing us.

One way we can encourage our children to say please and thank you is to use it consistently ourselves when we are speaking to them. I know it might feel a little over the top, but we can thank them too for saying please and thank you – 'Oh, thank you so much for saying please, that is very kind' – with a big smile of appreciation towards them. We can explain to them that saying please and thank you is a lovely way of showing other people that we care about them and respect them. They learn best through modelling and become more internally motivated as they realise this is meaningful in their relationship with us and with others.

Helping them with boundaries

We might need to be proactive in teaching these children that other people's moods, words and behaviour are *not* always something to do with them. This is an important life lesson that we can help them with. We can teach them how to be more boundaried with their emotions and hearts. It makes sense that they internalise other people's words because that is the way children make sense of the world. They relate everything back to themselves, and it takes time for them to learn that not everything is about them or their fault.

We can teach them that sometimes people say things that are unkind because they don't feel good inside. That when people are scared, sad, feel embarrassed or angry they might take their emotions out on someone else. That sometimes the way people cope with their painful feelings is by lashing out and being unkind to someone else. It's not that we are teaching them to excuse unhelpful behaviour, but we are helping them begin to see that other people's words and actions are not their fault. This can be hard for us as parents if we worry about being judged or if we don't want to offend others. You might relate to this if you tend to jump towards asking your child what they did wrong or can be quick to blame them in situations. Let's look at a conversation John has after school to make sense of this.

> *John is a ten-year-old boy who has just finished school for the day. His teacher, Linda, came into school feeling upset after an argument she had with her partner. Linda was feeling understandably stressed and knew she was outside her own window of tolerance. John, a sensitive child, was playing a game of cards at the back of the room with his friend Tom. The two boys didn't hear Linda calling their names to stop and join the class for maths. Frustrated and tired of feeling like no one was listening to her, Linda vocalised her disappointment in how disrespectful the two boys were being. Linda asked John and Tom for their copies and wrote a note home to their parents. John got a fright*

and felt upset, as he would never want to disrespect his teacher. He felt a lump gather in his throat and worried he would also be in trouble at home.

When John arrives home his parents are angry with him about the note. They quiz him about the situation in class and insinuate he clearly did something wrong to warrant a note home. John tries to explain but his parents have stopped listening. John goes up to his room and feels very down for the rest of the evening.

Now, of course there are going to be times we are not properly attuned with our children. The situation above is hard, I know, because so often our first reaction might be 'Oh no, what did you do?' – especially for those of us who feel anxious when other people are upset. We need to be really mindful of this, though, and practise taking a neutral and compassionate perspective, breathing deeply a few times ourselves before we come up with our own judgements and conclusions. We know from the research that these children need above-average levels of attunement, which is our ability as parents to understand and respond sensitively to their emotional needs. So even though we might have the best intentions, if there are too many occasions where they feel unheard, misunderstood or invalidated, it may begin to impact their mental health. This is never blaming anyone – it's all so hard, especially if it is our go-to response because that is how we were parented! These cycles get passed down so easily from generation to generation.

In an ideal situation, what we could do here instead is take the time to listen to John and hear his side of the story. We could validate his feelings and be compassionate towards the fright he experienced and the upset he is feeling. We could then practise taking the compassionate perspective with John about what was happening for his teacher.

'So, it sounds like you and Tom were playing cards when Linda was trying to start the class. I wonder how you think she might have been feeling, John? I know you mentioned she seemed a little stressed already that morning.'

'I know, Mom, but we didn't do anything wrong.'

'I hear you and I'm sorry you got a fright. I really hope you're okay. It sounds like Linda came into school already feeling a little stressed, and then feeling like you and Tom were ignoring her might have made her feel sad. Sometimes when people are stressed one more little thing just feels like too much.'

'Yeah, I suppose. I don't know what to do and I'm worried she hates me now.'

'I wonder could you write her a note to explain that you hadn't heard her and that you are sorry she was upset by that?'

'Okay, I'll do that.'

ON FEELING MISUNDERSTOOD

Of course, these conversations won't always go as smoothly as this one. Sometimes our sensitive souls (adults included) can feel very hurt if they are misunderstood. They might feel angry and upset towards the other person for not giving them the benefit of the doubt. This is where we, as parents, need to really work on putting ourselves in their shoes to be able to empathise with them. I have worked with so many sensitive children who cope with this by withdrawing from the other and by becoming silent and dismissive of them. They might think, 'Fine. If you are going to talk to me like that then you are not safe. I am not making any effort anymore.'

The difficulty here is that they don't yet understand that not everyone conducts themselves so carefully and thoughtfully – that we are imperfect humans who all react in unhelpful ways sometimes. They need to be extra mindful of practising forgiveness and letting things go. I don't mean every situation needs forgiveness, but for the most part, we can teach them that other people react, and it doesn't mean they don't still care about them just as much. If they feel frustrated, one of the best ways to help them is by giving them the opportunity to let it all out. Shout how angry they are from the rooftops if they want. Hit some pillows, go for a run, jump up and down or whatever physical exercise helps them let it out – just give them the space to release it! We should be mindful of trying to fix anything or trying to change their perspective, rather allowing the emotion to be really felt.

When we are helping our younger children cope with feeling misunderstood, it's a good idea to be careful of the language we use in putting words on their experience. While helping them name their emotions is hugely helpful, we need to remind ourselves to stay curious around this. If they are having a hard time and don't have the words to explain what is happening and we say, 'Oh, you're just hungry' or 'Oh, you're just tired', we might cause further upset and lead to them feeling misunderstood. Instead, we could change our language a little to 'Aw, hey, something has really upset you. I wonder is it because you are tired?' They might say no and continue letting out their upset. It's a good idea to respond by saying, 'Okay, it's not that. I'm sorry, love, something is upsetting you and I'm not sure what it is, but I'm here.'

Our deep-feeling children have such a longing to feel connected to and understood by those around them, especially us. Understanding the why behind their behaviour can be enormously helpful but we won't always be able to do this. Sometimes it is just a culmination of lots of stressors throughout the day, and their outflow of emotion is a wise release from their little bodies. Being a supportive presence and empathic witness to their pain and tensions is regulating for their nervous system and helps them feel seen and understood.

CHAPTER 8

Navigating painful emotions

Sadness can be a familiar emotion for a sensitive soul. Feeling the world deeply and noticing how painful life can be sometimes, and experiencing grief, loss, feeling excluded, rejection and being misunderstood can evoke feelings of sadness and loneliness. We can't shield our children from this, but we have enormous potential to help them when they go through challenging times.

Sadness

Annie is a sensitive nine-year-old who has a very close friend in school called Hannah. She loves Hannah so much, and the two girls do everything together. Daisy is another classmate whom Hannah has started to become friendly with recently. Annie notices Daisy doesn't seem to want to get to know her but makes it very obvious she wants to play with Hannah. Daisy hasn't said or done anything 'mean' necessarily, but she subtly ignores Annie by never engaging her in conversation and only making eye contact with the others when they are in a group.

One day Annie goes into school and overhears Daisy talking about the birthday party she is having in a few weeks. Her voice becomes quieter as Annie approaches, and she makes a 'shush' sound to the rest of the group. Annie, feeling confident on this occasion, says, 'Oh cool, Daisy, did I hear you're having a party?' Daisy smiles. Annie notices this smile doesn't reach her eyes when she answers, 'Oh yes, I am. It's a small sleepover so I'm only inviting my closest friends. Sorry about that, I hope you understand!' Annie feels a little lump in her throat as she replies with, 'Oh, that's cool. I hope you have a great time.' Annie looks towards Hannah and notices Hannah immediately looks down at the floor. Annie excuses herself to go to the bathroom and leaves the group.

This is a familiar story, I am sure, for many of you reading this book. Friendships can be tricky at the best of times, and stories like this one are a common occurrence as complex dynamics play out. This is sadly just a part of life and of growing up. The difficulty here is that a sensitive child will often experience these dynamics as particularly painful. Their depth of processing and empathy means that the sadness they experience here weaves in very deep.

And unfortunately, we can't fix this for them. Those of us who are more practical will likely either a) want them to move on and forget about it or b) want to do something about it. Sometimes parents want to get involved by speaking to the other child's caregiver and advocate for our child to be included. But neither of these options are very helpful for our child. Telling her to move on won't work, as the weight of being excluded is already heavy in her heart. Getting involved is also a risky game. The likelihood is that even if Annie was invited to the party, Daisy would feel resentful, and this would possibly cause more pain for Annie overall. Daisy may begin to laugh about this with peers or say how 'weird' it is that Annie is demanding to come to her party. She might say that Annie is only coming because her parents made her extend the invitation and laugh about 'how embarrassing' that is.

This situation might also bring up our own memories of feeling left out. Our children often evoke our own childhood wounds, which is why it's so painful for us to watch our children go through something similar. We might over-emphasise how hurtful a situation is and collapse into hopelessness alongside them. We might tell them to stay away from Daisy and to accept that Hannah is no longer a close friend. Although we are often so well intentioned when we meet our children in their sadness, we may inadvertently make them feel more upset about the situation. It is a careful balance between witnessing our child's sadness and not becoming consumed by it too. This is especially difficult for those of us who are more sensitive, as we experience their hurt feelings on a physiological level. When this happens, we lose access to that rational part of our brain that can remind us this is different than before and that hopefully our child will be okay.

The most helpful thing Annie's parents can do for her here is to be a soothing witness to her tears. Watching a sensitive child in pain is often incredibly upsetting. They feel this sadness so viscerally that it can be frightening to see the depth of this, and we can worry about what this means for them in life. We might feel concerned about their ability to cope. Here is where understanding their mind can be so empowering for us and them. I always tell parents to try not to feel too afraid of their child's pain. When life is hard, sensitive people feel it ten-fold. This means that what you see might seem extreme, but it is often in the experiencing of the emotion that we can move through it.

This means just allowing your child to be. Let them feel exactly how they are and be a kind and compassionate sturdy tree beside them, remembering that we are not there to fix it but rather to be a guide towards how to help it ease. These are the times they need us the most, so we might make an extra effort to spend time with them. Making them a little self-soothe box could be a kind gesture, with some cosy socks, teddies if they like them, maybe a figure of their favourite superhero, or simply a little card reminding them how special they are. Stories are such a powerful way of helping them feel less alone, so you could tell them a story about how you experienced something similar and that you remember how painful it was. We can look through books with them about similar situations and talk about how the main character coped. As they are prone to feeling 'stuck' in their sadness, we might have to actively help them here by validating their experience *and* showing them that they can do this, that we believe in them. We can remind them just how great a person they are, how lucky anyone is to be their friend and that we need to trust that it will all fall into place. Resilience builds slowly as these children experience the world, and the number-one buffer in helping them combat life's challenges is our unwavering support.

Trust

There are, of course, times when we will have to become involved. If your child is being repeatedly left out or bullied by peers, sitting down with their teacher to explain the particular situation and make a plan for how you are going to address the bullying in line with the school's anti-bullying policy will be important. Bullying can have a lasting impact on our child's emotional and physical well-being, and the ideal scenario is to involve our child with us in the process of dealing with it. Trust is such an important factor in our life with these children. We want them to be able to talk to us about anything and to know they can trust us with their feelings. This means that, where possible, we involve them in the decision about talking to other parents or to their teachers. I know that won't always be an option, and sometimes we will need to intervene without their approval. In these cases, we need to be mindful of the repair with them. We need to explain clearly why we have breached their confidence. We might explain how much we love them and, although it might be hard for them to understand right now, making sure the bullying is put to an end is extremely important.

Trust is sometimes overlooked in parenting, as we are the parent, and they are the child. We can forget just how intuitive they are and how much they pick up on. Trust is a vital part of the parent–child dynamic in building the secure attachment relationships with them that we discussed in chapter five. As discussed in chapter two, attachment is the relationship a child forms with a caregiver, where they seek comfort, nurture, soothing and protection. A secure attachment develops when the child learns that they can depend on their caregivers to meet their needs for safety, security, love and acceptance. This complex process deepens and develops over thousands of interactions in the relationship between caregiver and child. Their trust in us becomes woven into their neurobiology over time. The importance of this is illustrated in Kyle's story below.

> *Kyle is a ten-year-old who is struggling academically in school. He works hard every night and puts huge pressure on himself to keep up with his peers. He is awaiting an assessment for dyslexia and is embarrassed that he might be 'different'. His parents are trying to normalise this, but Kyle is not ready to hear it. He holds himself to very high standards and fitting in is important to him. He knows the boys in his class laugh behind Joseph's back because he has a diagnosis of dyspraxia. His peers would never say anything to Joseph's face, but Kyle knows they view him as 'different', and as a result he has never been fully accepted as part of the gang. Kyle's parents are well intentioned but can't understand why Kyle is being so 'over the top' about this assessment. Kyle has sat down with them both and pleaded with them not to tell anyone about*

it. He made them promise and explained why he felt so strongly about this.

A few days later Kyle was coming downstairs after playing on his Xbox. His parents had friends over, and he could hear their conversation loud and clear before he reached the last step. The hairs on his arms stood up as he overheard them laughing. 'It's ridiculous he doesn't want anyone to know. Like, he's very clearly dyslexic and you would swear this was the end of the world! He's embarrassed in front of his friends – it's all just so childish.' He could hear their friends agree and dismiss Kyle's feelings as 'dramatic'. This wasn't the first time his parents had broken his trust like this. He has overheard them numerous times telling other family members and friends about difficult situations he has experienced despite always asking them not to. Kyle makes the decision there and then that they can't be trusted. He pulls back from them and from then on keeps any worries to himself.

If you are reading this and worrying you have damaged your relationship with your child, I hope the rest of this paragraph will ease any stress! It is true that sensitive children are more likely to hold on to these painful memories and be much more cautious in their interactions with people who hurt them. It is also true that we can work on repair if we have inadvertently (and humanly) made a mistake and betrayed their trust. Modelling being able to apologise and talk about these mistakes is such a huge help for these kids. We can slowly build their trust again by being mindful of their privacy when something is important to them. Over time, this helps them come back into connection with us and understand that we are fallible too. Being genuine in our apology and taking responsibility can help build towards re-establishing trust. We can also practise really listening to our child's feelings when they tell us how much we let them down or betrayed them, being mindful not to use any 'but' phrases or minimise their upset. How we behave in those moments also teaches them how to respond when they make a mistake too. Modelling being open to accepting feedback and really listening is so helpful for our relationships with our children on so many levels.

Grief

We are all scared of succumbing to the depths of sadness we experience during grief, and sometimes we feel like we *can't* do it, especially when we are looking after children and don't have the option of falling apart completely. I have worked with remarkable parents who have gone through so much loss. Understandably, they say they feel like they did fall apart and could not be present as a parent for a certain time. They often experience huge guilt about this and worry about its implications. Please try to remember that life can be so full of love, but part of that love is loss, which means life can be messy, heartbreaking and full of despair. Humans are resilient, and if you look at our history and our evolution you will be reminded that we can find beauty again from even the darkest of places. If you read Edith Eger's or Viktor Frankl's stories from Auschwitz, you will see that even in the most horrifying circumstances, these incredible humans found meaning and love. So when we go through difficult times, or if our children have gone through times when we were not present or experienced suffering themselves, we can always help them find their light. We can also always find our way back to each other through showing our vulnerability and our care.

My biggest piece of advice in helping a sensitive child to deal with grief is, once again, to allow their experience to be. We need to be mindful about the fact that grieving will look different for all of us. Some children will want to bottle their sadness inside and let the tears flow when they are alone. Some children will need us so much more and will want to talk about the person or animal they have lost. Some will respond to their sadness with anger and push us away. Our younger children might experience regression in skills like using the toilet or sleep, and we might see their separation anxiety increase. Their behaviour might become more challenging as they process the swirl of grief inside their body. Just know that all of this is okay. We can become the compassionate holders of their broken hearts by being a comforting witness to their hurt.

Grief shows up in some unexpected ways with our highly sensitive children, which might feel confusing for us. I mentioned this in our chapter about empaths, but some children have a strong sense of 'right and wrong' and often grieve for those less fortunate in our society. They pick up on things they hear in the news, and when they hear about war and the devastation our fellow humans have to endure, they carry the weight of that with them. Something these big-hearted children will teach us, if we listen closely, is how 'the other' does not feel like something separate to them. It is not our fault, but sadly our more individualistic cultures have conditioned us to think more about our own lives than understand we are all part of the one world. We are all connected, and our children may grieve for the other as they feel connected to the world as a whole. This is a beautiful thing and, if possible, something we can help empower them with.

As I mentioned in chapter six, when the world feels out of control, one thing that really helps these kids is doing things that are in their control. They might grieve for the planet and become passionate about climate change. They might be heartbroken about what happens to animals and feel strongly about not eating something that has been alive. They might grieve for lost animals with no home or those who have been abandoned. If our lifestyle is different and we have not necessarily reflected much on these issues, it might feel confusing or frustrating to have a child who feels so strongly about them.

It can be an incredible gift to meet them in their interests and their passions, and there's no more important time to do this than when they are grieving for the 'other'. This shows them we want to help and that, while our values might look slightly different, we want to learn from them and nurture theirs. This helps them feel a sense of control in a world that feels frightening and unpredictable. It gives them a sense of agency, allowing them to give back and feel like they are doing their part in healing a sometimes cruel and unfair world. We might need to remind ourselves, too, not to laugh at their grief or tell them it is silly, which might feel hard if it seems 'over the top' to us. Let's have a look at Nya's story to illustrate this.

> Nya is a three-year-old who adores animals. She asks her father to read her books about animals every night before bed. Her big eyes light up with wonder as she learns all about bees, snails and bugs. She loves stories about dogs and cats and is fascinated by what feel like other mystical creatures from the animal kingdom. Story after story, that deep-thinking wonderful brain of hers soaks it all in. Her dreams are full of excitement and adventure as she lives alongside the animals in her stories.
>
> One day Nya is sitting in the living room watching what looks like a baby wasp that must have got lost. Nya is deep in thought about how to help the little wasp get home to her friends. She is in awe at the young wasp's beauty and is enjoying listening to the soft buzzing sound she is making. Before she knows what is happening, her mother hits the wasp with a cloth. Nya watches in disbelief as the wasp falls to the floor. Her mother, unaware of the impact of this on Nya, says, 'Thank god! How do they keep getting in?' Nya's eyes fill with tears, and she shouts, 'How could you!' at her mom and buries her head in her hands.
>
> Nya's mother laughs and says, 'Oh, Nya, stop being so ridiculous! It's only a wasp and it could have stung you.' Nya spends the next few hours crying and feels overwhelmed with grief about the baby wasp who will never get home.

This is a common example of what can happen to our sensitive souls and how their grief may feel confusing for us. This is why it can be particularly helpful to take time to understand their interests. One thing that might help here is having a spiritual goodbye for the wasp. You could bury it in the garden and encourage your child to talk about their feelings. We can show them that, although there is death, there is also so much life still here and help them continue to see this beauty.

I can hear the 'Ah, here …' response coming from those of you who are more practical! I get it, believe me, and my best friends would laugh with love at how OTT this might feel. Bear with me, though! Because if these children are here to teach us something and to remind us that we all matter, then nurturing this side of them can only be a good thing. We could really do with more love and care in this world that can be hard and cold. So while you might cringe internally, try to give it a go and watch their connection to you grow too. Our children might know we don't necessarily feel the same way, but they will appreciate our time and thoughtfulness.

Siblings

We hear so much about sensitive children and their big hearts but sometimes it can feel quite the opposite when siblings are involved. This can be so challenging to manage as a parent. It might help to reflect on this through the eyes of a child. If we remember that we are their whole world, then it makes sense that a new arrival might evoke feelings of sadness in them. Let's have a look at Liam's story.

Liam is a five-year-old who has been so excited to meet his baby sister. He tells everyone who will listen that his mom has a baby in her tummy. He says he can't wait to show all his friends and feels so proud of himself that he will be her big brother. He is a very intuitive child and feels older than his years. He immediately corrects anyone who calls him a small boy and explains he is in fact a very 'big boy'.

When Liam's sister Lisa arrives, he is full of joy. He is fascinated by her little hands and toes and wants to give her as many hugs as he can. He notices his parents are constantly telling him to be careful and to be gentler with the baby. His little mind feels confused with this, as he is only trying to be kind. He begins to notice his parents don't have as much time to play anymore. He feels a little lump in his throat every time they say 'later' when he wants to play superheroes. Everyone who calls to the house seems to just want to look at Lisa, and sometimes they forget to even say hello to him. He looks around the room at his parents smiling lovingly at Lisa and has a heavy feeling in his chest. Reminding himself he is a 'big boy', he pushes that feeling away and immerses himself in his toys.

The weeks go on and not much changes. He notices his parents are cross and seem so tired all the time. He feels an anger stirring inside at Lisa. She is the reason his whole world has changed, and he has decided he does not like her anymore. He asks his parents can they send Lisa back. Every night in bed he wonders what this feeling is

> inside. He has a pain in his tummy and remembers his book about the lonely whale. Liam has a pain where his heart is and realises he feels exactly like the lonely whale in his story. With a sinking feeling, he closes his heavy eyes and drifts off to sleep.

This will be a familiar feeling for some children when a sibling arrives. Their whole world is turned upside down very quickly, and they notice their life before is gone. This will likely evoke feelings of sadness and loneliness in their hearts. Try not to worry too much if you have recently added to your family or are hoping to in the future. Like any change, it will just take some time. There are a few things that can really help our sensitive children navigate this and some things that might make the transition a little more difficult.

With the best intentions, we might really encourage our child to love the new baby. This makes sense – we want this transition to go smoothly and for our child to feel okay. We want to nurture this relationship, so we tell them how lucky they are to have a little sister or brother. We might assume they love their new sibling without taking the time to acknowledge the very real loss they are experiencing: the loss of their family unit as they knew it. We might forget they are grieving their life before. We might say things like: 'You love your little sister – you have to be nice to the baby' or 'You're the big brother now – you have to look after your sister'. While this is well intentioned, we often forget they are still only small too. This can be particularly easy to forget with our wise souls who seem older than their years. They might speak like a far older chld, and as a result we forget that, developmentally, their little minds will find this situation very hard to navigate.

They are often left feeling confused, as their inner world might sound like:

- 'But I thought I was the baby?'
- 'I don't like the baby – why do I have to be nice?'
- 'They keep saying I love the baby, but I don't. Maybe they will be angry with me now and won't love me anymore.'
- 'I feel so sad. They don't seem to have as much time for me anymore.'
- 'What's wrong with me? I am supposed to love the baby, but I just feel angry.'

While they might not have the language to express this, the feeling might be the same. Ideally, we help them with this by not expecting too much from them. We might narrate their inner world for them by saying something like: 'I know you might feel sad now that your sister is here – it's okay if you do. Whatever you feel is okay. I miss all our time together too. I love you so much – you will always be my baby too.'

We will probably see some unhelpful behaviours as they process the change, so we should try to discover what need they are trying to communicate underneath the behaviour. For example, if your older child starts hitting the baby, you would safely remove the baby and then say something like: 'Oh no, love, hitting really hurts and I can't let you hit your sister. I see you are frustrated; I know and I'm so sorry. I wish I could play with you now too. I know this is hard for you. Why don't you bring me over a book I can read to you while I finish feeding your sister? And I can't wait to play with you when I'm finished.'

And where possible, build in as many opportunities for one-to-one connection as we can. I know that is difficult when we are stretched thin and exhausted ourselves. I felt very guilty and sad myself in the early days while I was navigating this with my sons. Our one-to-one connection was little pockets of time spread through the day. This looked like hugs, tickles, cosy time on the couch together while his little brother slept and constant reminders of how special he was and how I understood his feelings. Try to go easy on yourselves and remember that these children are resilient too. When we really allow their emotional experience to be, they feel seen and understood, even if the situation is still the same.

Something else to keep an eye out for is if your child begins communicating their needs through their sibling. I have observed my eldest doing this recently. He has been explaining to me that 'I can't give up the bottles, Mommy, because Ollie will feel lonely if I do'. 'Ollie told me he wants me to keep my soother too.' 'I better stay home today as Ollie said he really misses me when I go to school sometimes.' Meanwhile his brother is completely unaware and busying himself with some truck or digger in the garden! If you are hearing this or noticing their needs being communicated in this way, I would encourage you to lean into it if possible. It is often their way of letting us know they are looking for a little more connection and soothing from us. They are most likely feeling apprehensive about a transition, or their separation anxiety is peaking, and they may be feeling embarrassed, thus their needs are communicated more indirectly. Often when we meet the need for more comfort, more reassurance and more safety, they feel surer and more confident in themselves to take little steps towards more independence.

It can be helpful to take a compassionate approach to sibling rivalry. You might be thinking, 'Seriously, Aoife? It's not easy to stay calm during fighting. They need strict boundaries!' I understand – I am exhausted trying to manage the sibling rivalry in our family a lot of the time. It is helpful to remind ourselves that while, yes, clear, kind and firm boundaries help, tuning into the need will pay off in the long run. This is because, unfortunately, their lack of impulse control makes it just as likely to happen again. Sometimes the child who is engaging in the not-so-helpful behaviour is the one who needs the most support. This usually looks like me jumping in between the two during a fight and trying my best to soothe both kids while helping them understand the impact of their behaviour on the other – holding the one who is hurt, while communicating to the culprit that I hear they need help too. I definitely do not get this right all the time, but when I do, I really see the benefits, not only in our connection but in the sibling relationship too, as there is no 'winner' in their eyes.

Sibling rivalry often ebbs and flows as they grow. It is understandable that they will feel jealous sometimes. If we practise being curious about their behaviour, it will often signal to us who needs a little more of our time. Take care of yourself too because it can evoke so much stress and guilt in us parents. Remind yourself that you have hopefully given them a best friend for life and that when the early years (which for myself and my sensitive sister lasted a very long time …) pass, eventually they get there and have the most special bond.

'Difference'

Some disabilities we can see, and some are less visible. We have a huge opportunity to help our children view disability as not something that is 'less than' but rather something that is wonderfully different. The world would be a very boring place if we were all the same.

It is crucial to model this early on for our children and to be mindful of the language we use when describing people who are 'different' to us. We should never talk about someone with a disability with sympathy. This sounds like: 'Aw, poor Tom, he's in a wheelchair. It's so sad – his poor parents must find it so hard.' Or say we see an autistic child stimming in the supermarket: we don't say 'don't look' or suggest that there is something wrong with this. Rather we can talk to our children about how we all use our voices and bodies in different ways when we are feeling excited and happy or stressed and overwhelmed. We might explain that some children use their voice loudly or move their body in a different way to communicate and this is all okay! No two of us are the same, and it's great to be curious about other people.

We can make an extra effort to read books that include people of all shapes, sizes, skin colours and using wheelchairs, crutches and so on. We can constantly explain that being different is a cool thing and encourage our children to be curious about this.

Our child's brain is like a sponge, and we have an enormous capacity to influence them. The beliefs we have about being 'different' have been passed down from generation to generation. It's not your fault if you feel anxious about this or about facilitating these discussions. So much of our thinking around being different is deeply engrained from ideological views that are outside of our conscious control.

One of the reasons this is so important is that by three months of age babies begin to show a preference for looking at faces similar to their caregivers and a preference for their own race. Children are trying to build their identities early on, and to do this they use perceptual similarities or dissimilarities. Research shows us that exposure to diversity can make other faces feel just as familiar as their own. This means that even if children live in areas without a lot of diversity, they should be shown pictures of people from different races and cultures. And for this reason, it is important to ask ourselves, how do we talk about people who look or communicate differently to us? How do we treat them?

We can explain that all families are different too, and that people have different sexualities and gender identities. These discussions are something we can actively encourage early on. My good friend and disabled activist Paddy Smyth says, 'It's okay to ask questions, it's okay to be interested. Often non-disabled people find it difficult to ask questions or feel like the disabled people are victims in some way. They might try to help the disabled person and overcompensate for their disability; however, the disabled person experiences that as that they are being treated differently. Disabled is not a dirty word. Disabled people sometimes are at a disadvantage and that is a part of their life.'

We can look at Laura's story to illustrate this.

> *Laura is a six-year-old who has cerebral palsy. Laura has difficulty articulating sounds clearly and her speech is slightly slurred. She is an incredible child who is so sensitive and has a very big heart. She loves making new friends and loves going to the playground to chat to the other children. Her curious mind loves the excitement of the hustle and bustle, and the sound of children squealing and laughing is like music to her ears. The swing is her favourite, and she could easily spend half an hour swinging in delight.*
>
> *Laura wants nothing more than to connect with the other children. She is highly intuitive and is acutely aware of every 'shush' a parent makes to their child who is staring or whisper to 'stop looking' in her direction. Her big heart feels incredibly sore every time this happens. She can't understand why people look away when they see her or why they look at her with sympathy. She loves life and, yes, she might be different, but she has always been this way and she loves who she is. Laura feels a deep sense of loneliness, as she is realising she does not fit in. This not fitting in is not due to her disability – it is due to how her disability is viewed by others. This breaks her family's heart, and they are becoming more anxious about the impact this will have on Laura's mental health.*

It is in our hands as a society to make this change and help Laura and those wonderful children like her feel connected, valued and welcome. Although we might mean well when we tell children to stop staring, we need to practise doing the opposite of this. We might say to our child who stares, 'Oh, wow. That's called a wheelchair. That helps that little girl move around. It has big wheels on it, just like the trucks you love. Why don't we go over and say hello?' Children are naturally curious so they will ask questions. Try not to worry about having the exact 'right' response. We are all always growing, and most people will appreciate our compassion and openness to learning about difference. The interesting thing about children is that they are usually not fazed by difference and just say 'oh, cool' once we explain. It is our bias and anxiety that can be passed down and influence how they interpret others who look or communicate differently.

None of us will get this right all of the time. I often struggle to find the right words and feel so anxious about saying the wrong thing. We can only do our best. We can be kind to ourselves too and remember we can help our children with this at any stage. We might sit down and explain to them that we have been doing a lot of reading and realise we have things to learn ourselves. We can invite them to learn alongside us, slowly changing our beliefs one day at a time, holding on to the power of the collective and how supportive we can be towards difference, empowering our children to do the same.

CHAPTER 9

Understanding our strong-willed children

While many of our sensitive children move through the world a little tentatively, our strong-willed sensitive kids are much more assertive about their needs. They tend to be more determined and crave their own independence. These children have the biggest hearts and are often fiercely passionate in their beliefs. They go after what they want, and if we can nurture these big-feeling children in the right way, we can help their spark turn into something truly magical. They often become leaders, and they are brave and authentically themselves.

Unfortunately, throughout their younger years, we can hear them referred to as our 'difficult' children. They are often described as 'bold' or 'stubborn', and their strong will is viewed through a negative lens. They know their own mind and often speak up for those who are being discriminated against, left out or bullied.

They are intense and persistent in their ideas and when communicating their needs. But they are not as sturdy as they might appear. They are sensitive and kind and are not immune from having their little spirits hurt.

A story about two sisters

The elder sister is a sensitive child who feels her emotions deeply. She is more cautious in her interactions and is often slow to warm in new environments and when meeting new people. She quickly notices when her behaviour is perceived through a negative lens and learns early on how to hide certain parts of herself. The younger is also a sensitive child who feels every emotion with intensity. She is what we call our 'spirited' or 'strong-willed' sensitive child. She is fiercely passionate in her beliefs and does not easily conform to rules or expectations. She knows her own mind and tends to challenge the status quo.

The elder child mostly internalises her emotions. She goes deep into her own inner world and copes with feelings like fear, sadness or shame by turning these emotions inward, igniting a self-critic that, for years to come, will believe it is helping her by keeping her in check. She is mostly easy to discipline and is amenable to teachers or other figures in authority. Her behaviour is commended in school but is often a challenge at home. Rather than internalise her emotions, the younger tends to externalise hers. She is not as easy to discipline and craves independence. Her feelings fly out of her body more quickly, and it does not take much to fire up her little amygdala (fight/flight/freeze/fawn response). She is easier to get into a 'power struggle' with, as she wants to feel understood and have a sense of choice and control.

The elder sister needs help to be her authentic self – to feel loved and accepted just as she is. She needs help in challenging the notion that being 'nice' is more important than using her voice and speaking her mind. She needs help when she is deep in her inner world to create meaning around the emotions she is experiencing, learning that other people's words or expectations are not a reflection of who she is. She needs to know that it's okay to mess up sometimes and that this is how we grow. The younger needs others to recognise her big feelings are a reflection of a big heart that feels so intensely. She needs to know that she is not 'bold' or 'defiant' and just needs some help in managing the swirl of emotions happening inside. Harsh discipline or punishment will only extinguish this little firecracker's spark. Flexibility in meeting her where she is at while gently holding loving limits will help her nervous system feel more at ease.

Both of these sensitive children experience the world in the same way: they have deep-processing brains and big hearts that feel every emotion to their core.

Their needs are the same.

Their behaviour is different.

Connection is always the answer.

Understanding behaviour

It is easy to fall into a more authoritarian role with strong-willed children and believe we have to 'show them who is the boss'. This is not our fault – it is from a conditioned belief that has been passed down from generation to generation. You might wonder why this is the case and why so many of us, along with our parents' generation, have grown up in this authoritarian style of discipline at home or in school. Thanks to pioneers in the fields of neuroscience, developmental psychology and psychiatry this is changing, but unfortunately much of our parenting advice has been heavily influenced by behaviourism. This is a psychological theory that suggests that behaviours are learned through conditioning and that behaviour can be modified by reinforcement and punishment. While behaviourism has made significant contributions to understanding learning and conditioning, it does not account for a child's unique brain development, attachment needs, sensory preferences or temperament or how all children have different timelines for their social and emotional development. Many parenting 'experts' in the 1990s and early 2000s taught parents how to engage in tactics for promoting obedience in their children rather than empowering parents to understand the science of a developing child's brain. This approach taught parents that their child's behaviour was stemming from 'boldness' or manipulation and is completely at odds with the research on child development. Parents, unfortunately, became more disconnected from their children, and parenting became more about who was in control. This was not easy for the parent of a strong-willed child and sadly often caused a rupture in the parent–child dynamic. While following this advice, we moved further away from understanding the neurobiology of a child's mind and what the research in developmental psychology and attachment theory shows us.

We were taught to overestimate a child's ability to understand cause and effect – meaning when we tell a child not to do something and they test the limits by doing it again, we were taught to interpret this as 'you are intentionally doing this to disobey me'. The reason we believed this is just a reflection of the previous generation of parenting. This advice has also made parenting feel so hard. It has led us to interpret challenging behaviour as a reflection on our parenting or of misbehaviour, without realising that these younger humans are acting mainly from their emotional brain. So much of what we believe to be 'bad behaviour' is often developmentally appropriate as they push boundaries and learn how to assert themselves and voice their needs. Pushing boundaries is a healthy part of development, where they learn what is appropriate and what is 'too much'. Our more spirited and determined children will push these boundaries more as they try to carve out their independence.

Examples of this style of parenting include viewing tantrums as attention-seeking and encouraging parents to ignore them and using 'time outs' as consequences for 'bad' behaviour and rewards for when children act in appropriate ways and comply. In one sense, we can see how this school of thought has been so popular because the reality is it works! Children are extremely adaptable, and we can often 'train' them to behave in certain ways. The risk here is that the more we do this the less understood and safe they feel. So while these strategies may work in the short term, they can lead to difficulties later on and disconnection in their relationship with us. While threatening and punishment may work with a younger child who depends on us for their survival, it will become a lot more difficult with a teenager who starts to fight back or who sadly may disengage from us entirely. This authoritarian form of discipline unfortunately often causes our children to feel anxious and unsafe in their attachment relationship with us. We should be building the foundations in them now to know that they can depend on us as they grow. This attachment relationship really is so important in helping them feel safe and protected and, most importantly, it builds their sense of self-worth.

Even if we have not been as attuned as we hoped we would be, we can begin repairing this with our children at any age. Research shows us that our brain continues to remodel itself in response to more positive experiences throughout our entire lives. So we can help our children create more helpful neural networks in their brain. One of the best ways to do that is through co-regulation.

When trying to help our more determined and strong-willed children, we might remind ourselves that we are not born with the ability to self-regulate. We learn how to regulate our emotions after years of co-regulation from our caregivers. This warm, understanding, repeated soothing will shape and build our later self-regulation skills. This is still hard for so many of us, myself included. You might relate to that feeling of sometimes 'flying off the handle' or becoming so overwhelmed that you feel like shouting (or, like me, do shout sometimes!). This is a continuing work in progress for all of us.

You might be wondering what this actually looks like in practice. Let's look at Holly's story to help us make sense of this.

Holly is a sensitive eight-year-old who feels every emotion with great intensity. When she feels regulated, she is a very loving and caring child. She has a quick wit and seems to have a sense of humour that is far beyond her years. She is so much fun and captivates anyone she meets. She is also a determined little soul! Her parents laugh anxiously when describing this, saying, 'Oh, Holly most certainly knows her own mind.' She can go from zero to a hundred in a matter of seconds, and her meltdowns cause her parents a huge amount of stress. They feel embarrassed about her behaviour, as they have been on the receiving end of many judgemental glances and comments.

The latest concern they have is why Holly reacts with such intensity to change. Most recently, her father handed Holly her cereal in a different bowl than usual. Her red bowl was in the dishwasher, so he used a blue bowl instead. Holly's face crumpled the moment he handed her the bowl as she threw it on the floor, screaming, 'No! Not that one! I don't like that one!' Her parents, at a loss for what to do, became tense and stressed, while her meltdown escalated so much that she wouldn't eat any breakfast. She said she felt sick and could not tolerate the thought of food.

Let's look at this from a psychological perspective and see how we might help Holly and her parents in this situation. Firstly, it is understandable that Holly's parents feel anxious. It is hard to navigate these big emotions when they feel so confusing.

It will be helpful here to be curious about Holly's behaviour.

We know that unexpected changes may be experienced as overwhelming for a child with heightened emotional awareness. Sensitive children may experience this as more stressful, pushing them out of their window of tolerance and into their threat system. In this case, Holly has found the unpredictability alarming, and on a physiological level, Holly's nervous system is interpreting this change of cereal bowl as unsafe. Her behaviour is being driven by her heightened sensitivity to environmental stimuli and it is not intentional. Her neurobiology is experiencing physiological differences that are influencing her behaviour. Threat reactions like this occur across three different levels: psychological, behavioural and physiological.

We also need to trust Holly when she says she feels sick, remembering that when we are stressed, upset or anxious our homeostasis is off-centre. When our sensitive children are in a state of alarm, their body is not functioning in sync anymore, which means that it can't carry on digesting food, and the adrenaline and cortisol flooding her body manifest as feeling sick. Holly's parents here might understandably respond by reprimanding her for throwing the bowl. We could go back to chapter two and the Three Rs here as a way of helping Holly's parents manage this situation, remembering that we need to help Holly regulate before we try and reason with her about throwing being an unhelpful response.

GIVE THEM A SENSE OF AGENCY AND CONTROL

I can't emphasise enough how helpful choice and control will be for you in parenting these passionate children. They feel everything with such intensity, and being told what to do is often something that sets off their little alarms. Once they have decided they need or want something, or don't want to do something, this is experienced as a fierce drive within their little nervous system. So when we come along as their parent and say no or hold a strict boundary, their amygdala feels under attack, and we watch in confusion as their little world seems to implode. Having compassion for them in these moments by reframing our understanding of their behaviour can help us feel much less activated by this. Giving them choices and helping them be part of any decision we make gives them a sense of agency and control in their life. If we approach boundaries with a strict 'no means no' or 'because I said so', it is likely to end up in a stressful situation for all involved.

What is much more helpful is saying something like: 'We have to turn off the TV now because it has been on for an hour. I know it's hard when you're enjoying your favourite show, but it's just that any longer gives us all a cranky head. You can choose what you would like to do next.' Another might be: 'No, love, Rian can't come over to play today because I have to work. I am sorry you are disappointed; I know you were really hoping he could. Rian can come next week, so let's make a plan for what we will do then.'

Small choices in our day-to-day help so much. For our younger children this might sound like: 'Would you like to wear your green coat or your red coat?' 'Would you prefer porridge or cereal today?' 'Would you like to brush your teeth now or get into your pyjamas first?' As they grow, it could be letting them pick their own clothes, what they would like to make for their lunch, the movie for a family movie night and so on. A great approach in parenting these children is to bring play into our lives as much as we can! For example, if a child is refusing to get dressed, we can pretend their socks are crocodiles and want to eat their feet. If a child is saying 'no way' to toothbrushing, we can pretend the toothbrush is a train and their teeth are the tracks. If a child is refusing to leave the house, we can play 'countdown' by opening our front door and pretend the space rocket is getting ready for launch in 'Ten – Do you hear that [makes noises]? Oh! the engines are on! Nine – oh wow, I hear the turbo blasters firing up [more silly noises]! We don't want to miss the launch. Eight! Ahh, we are running out of time, where are our shoes??' and so on. Putting on some music and doing silly dances can be a great mood-shifter for the whole family too! There are many ways we can turn battles into 'fun' – there are some brilliant resources in the back of this book (page 271).

Our biggest goal when parenting these children is to help them feel connected, have their inner world validated and their feelings heard. I can't stress how helpful this will be for them as they grow up and begin to put words on their experience. When their relationship with us is strong and they learn they can depend on us to meet their needs, this helps them feel connected to us, which in turn often makes parenting less stressful. They become more motivated to engage in behaviours that align with our values when they feel supported, valued and understood. Try not to give up when it feels like things aren't working and trust the process of love and connection. They might not be children who comply early on, and we often need a little help in recognising this is okay. It's fine that these little firecrackers know their own mind, and over time, when our connection is strong, they grow into the most wonderful people. We can help them be mindful and reflect on how their behaviour might make us or others feel when they act passionately because of their own needs and wants, remembering that when they are being driven from this place, they likely have tunnel vision of their own point of view and may need help from us in learning how to consider others' thoughts and feelings. Don't assume they are not kind or empathic because of their fiery side. These kids feel their emotions to their core – they just sometimes get lost in their inner world that is full of determination.

> *Cora was most definitely not an 'easy' child. Her determination and intense emotions resulted in many challenges growing up. She was fiercely driven by her own needs, and although her parents knew she was a sensitive soul, her depth of emotion often resulted in head-to-head arguments. They worried about her behaviour and what kind of person she would become. They thought she may turn into a 'selfish' adult.*
>
> *In fact, she became the exact opposite. Looking back, they wish they had given her more choice and flexibility. They realise their 'no means no' approach only exacerbated this sensitive soul's feelings of being misunderstood. Cora is now in her late teens and is described by friends and family as one of the most gentle, caring and empathic*

people they know. She recently won an award at school for being the 'kindest person in the year'. She has such a huge heart, mixed with strength of character, passion and determination.

It is fascinating to watch a child like Cora grow up in the world. Not only does she care so much about others, but she has an inner force to be reckoned with that advocates for those who need support. If you are lucky enough to have someone like Cora in your life, you will have a pretty special relationship.

Hang on in there if you have a little firecracker like Cora. Adjust your expectations if you can, and trust in the power of empathy and connection with your child. Try and reframe their 'defiance' as an understandable need they have for more freedom and choice in their life. When we lean into this as best we can, we often see the more challenging behaviours decrease. A good question to ask ourselves if we are feeling frustrated is: 'What can I give my child more control over right now?'

OUR STRONG-WILLED CHILDREN OFTEN NEED SOME FLEXIBILITY

We are used to living in a fast-paced environment where we don't often have the luxury of slowing down. However, our strong-willed children will often force us to slow down and have some degree of flexibility in our lives. If we fight against this, the power struggles can cause us a lot of stress.

Often children feel frustrated when they haven't mastered a

new skill yet. Think of when they are learning to walk, talk, use the toilet, ride a bike, read, write and so on. While they are building a sense of mastery over these things, they often feel overwhelmed, and their frustration tolerance is low. When things feel out of control, our children will try to control the controllable. This is especially the case for our strong-willed little ones who are craving independence. This often translates to more challenging behaviour that can feel confusing to parents. During these times we might be more flexible with them.

I have worked with many parents who decide to pull back on certain rules, like sleeping at a particular time, homework being completed before play or dinner being had at the table, and have seen a huge shift in their child's behaviour. I know we worry, 'Well, if I do it once then they will think it's the norm from now on' and I hear you. I have been stuck in this cycle myself many times. We often feel like we have gone backwards and are facing another battling climb back up.

But when we meet them where they are at and are flexible during certain times (rather than keeping to rigid rules about what they 'should' be doing), they will feel understood and validated. So, for example, if our children are exhausted after a long day and mealtimes are a battle, try to take the pressure off by leaving their dinner for them and allowing them to eat it when they feel hungry. If for some reason they are really refusing to go asleep, consider allowing them to sit beside you on the couch while you read your book or watch TV. It's not that I recommend doing this all of the time, but providing them with a sense of being heard about what they need at times can be so helpful.

When we get the sense they are ready for it again, we can gently explain why we will try to have our dinner at the table again and why it's important we go asleep earlier. Explain that you're not trying to be mean: you want to eat with them because you love sitting beside them, and you want them to go asleep because you want their body and mind to feel good in the morning. Feeling tired, too much sugar, too much TV and so on can give all of us a 'cranky head'. While they might be unhappy with our rules, they often understand more than we realise and will in time appreciate our loving limits.

A reactivity guide

Something that helps me in dealing with reactivity is wondering what is going on for my child in these moments. I have a checklist I run through first in my head. This is just a simple screening list but one that is often overlooked. It sounds like:

- Are they seeking connection with me? How am I feeling? Could they be picking up on my stress or do they need more of my attention?
- Are they tired? What has their sleep hygiene looked like over the last few days?
- Are they feeling nourished? What has their food intake been? Might they be hungry or have they had certain foods (maybe lots of sugar) that have contributed to a stressed nervous system?
- Are they feeling sick? Might they have a pain in their tummy or, for our younger children, is teething a contributor?

- Have they had enough fresh air and movement? Could this stress be stemming from a lack of activity and a body that needs to move more?
- Are they overwhelmed? Have they been on the go a lot over the last few days? Are we seeing a collapse into exhaustion from doing too much?
- Has there been any change recently? Could they be responding to stress in relation to changes in our life?

There are more things we could add to this list, but running through this brief checklist helps me think about their reactivity. It is much easier to manage when I am able to say, 'Oh, this makes sense'.

I know I make that sound easy but, believe me, I understand how stressful it can be to keep yourself regulated when your child is having a meltdown. Recently, one of my children had a very intense meltdown over the wrong yogurt. I ran through my checklist and realised that the unpredictability (the wrong yogurt) along with too much activity that day had set off a little alarm. We had already gone to the playground and the supermarket and spent time visiting friends and family. I did my best to co-regulate with him by taking a deep breath and reminding myself that this was not his fault. Then I empathised with him by saying, 'Aw, I know, love, you were hoping for the other yogurt and they are all gone. I understand. I'm so sorry you're upset.'

I won't pretend I felt completely calm as the meltdown continued – I felt like I was at the very edge of my window of tolerance and found it very difficult to stay regulated. Please know this is understandable and normal. It is so hard to stay calm sometimes, even when we can empathise with the situation. In these moments, we need to practise being our own best friend and say, 'Hey, you're okay. I am here. This is hard but it will pass. What do you need right now that might help you cope?' Ear plugs are a gamechanger in parenting and can help us to come down from, say, an 8/10 stress, where we are about to snap at our child, to maybe a 6/10, where we feel we can breathe again and think about what might de-escalate the situation. I will talk more about minding our own sensory profile in the next chapter.

It's helpful to remember too in these moments that it is rarely just about the yogurt, or about the bowl in Holly's example. It is likely lots of little stressors that have built up throughout the day and then one more thing is just too much. You might relate to that in yourself too. You might be able to regulate yourself for most of the day, despite numerous things that were stressful. And then you come home, and the house is turned upside down or someone says something to annoy you, and you go from zero to a hundred in a matter of seconds. It is likely not just about that one thing but the build-up of lots of little challenging situations throughout the day. And if that is hard for us to manage, you can imagine how much more difficult it is for our children who are still only learning how to calm their little nervous systems.

The importance of co-regulation

Sometimes, we can do everything 'right', but our child has been tipped so far into their fight/flight/freeze/fawn response that we just have to help them let it all out. What children need in these moments will look different for all of them, as every child is unique. Some children want a hug while they cry as loud as their little lungs can manage. Some children will want to run around and may try to bang their heads off the floor or the walls. If this happens, we need to follow them around as best we can and try to prevent them from hurting themselves. Some older children might want to go to their room and scream at you to leave them alone. If so, we might just need to softly tell them we are here for them when they are ready. This can be confusing, as some children will just need a little breather alone to regulate themselves enough to then want our soothing presence. Others will tell us to go away and shout, but all they really want is a hug or for us to be in the room with them telling them we get it. So it involves a little trial and error on our behalf as we figure out what works for them.

As they get older, when the meltdown has ended (not at the time) we can ask them what helps them in those moments of overwhelm. We can explain their brain and nervous system to them again, normalising what happens for all of us when we are flooded with stress hormones. 'Imagine your brain is like a busy playground [adapt this depending on age]. There is so much going on in this playground and sometimes it all starts to feel a bit too much in there [point to your head]. When this happens, our brain feels a little stressed and tries its best to calm down. It does this by releasing lots of feelings and energy through our mouths and our bodies. It's pretty cool that our brains do this to help us, but I know it can feel confusing at the time.' Keep in mind that they may be hard on themselves after the meltdown has passed, so making them feel less alone with this really helps them. It also helps to remember what is happening in their brain – we just need to remind ourselves that, during these periods of reactivity, they have lost access to their thinking, rational brain.

An important piece in helping them to regulate is tuning in to our tone of voice. There is fascinating research on how influential our tone can be. (If you have a child who is deaf or hard of hearing, don't worry, as we can convey tone with our body language and our facial expressions too.) This research shows that a soothing voice reaches our child's physiology. Also being gentle in their presence is shown to help regulate our child's stress system on a brain level. When we respond to children (or anyone in our life) with calm and soothing non-verbal and verbal communication, the human body responds by regulating itself. If we speak in loud, stressed or angry tones, whoever we are communicating with will experience a stress reaction on a physiological level and get pushed into their fight/flight/freeze/fawn.

You might be thinking, 'I do that, and it doesn't help'. I hear you. We have been led to believe that we should see quick results from 'parenting tips'. However, this type of attunement and co-regulation does not mean that the meltdown won't happen again and in the exact same way it did before. We might then think, 'This isn't working – surely I am doing something wrong'. I understand how exhausting and frustrating this might feel. The reality is that you are unlikely to see 'results' that are identifiable quickly, but that does not mean you are doing the wrong thing. Some of our children will take years before they are able to access their own self-regulatory networks. This is completely developmentally appropriate but not something we have a lot of information on.

So if you have a spirited sensitive child, you need to remember that their window of tolerance is smaller than their peers'. And thus it might take them longer to regulate, and their meltdowns may continue for longer too. This does not mean you are doing anything wrong, and continuously providing them with safe and predictable co-regulation will help wire their neural networks to do it themselves as they grow.

Understanding big feelings behind closed doors

Something that often confuses parents is why their child appears to be able to regulate with friends, in school or in other social settings but feels so difficult to manage at home. This question understandably makes parents believe they must be the problem. And again, while we do have a lot of influence in helping soothe their stress response, often they are 'letting it all out' with us as we are their safest people.

I recently received an email from a parent saying they were at a loss with their sensitive child. They explained how their child was excelling in school, had many friends and every parent–teacher meeting could not be more positive about their kind, empathic and caring child. But at home, this parent was seeing the very opposite. Their child seemed so angry all of the time and was verbally unkind to the whole family. They explained how his siblings had stopped wanting to play with him and how the parents were unable to 'keep their cool' anymore – their patience had worn out and they were completely depleted. They explained how they would have weeks or even months sometimes of their son being very calm and loving, but it's like a switch would flip and he would have a lot of outbursts, physically and verbally, along with a lot of negative self-talk.

I know I keep reiterating this, but it is understandable that these parents are finding this difficult to manage. Being on the receiving end of outbursts of anger is upsetting for any of us. Often our own childhood wounds become activated here too – we are only human. Verbal and physical outbursts can evoke such painful feelings in us, depending on our own life history. It is also deflating to receive this when you are doing everything you can to help them. So many parents I work with end up feeling like they are walking on eggshells with their child. They feel sad and often resentful towards them, as they feel so defeated by this challenging behaviour. While it is important to be boundaried around verbal and physical outbursts, we really need to remember these outbursts are stemming from a distressed nervous system.

How to manage our response

On many occasions I have reverted into a childlike state myself in response to challenging behaviour. Rather than staying regulated and remembering it is developmentally normal, I felt flooded with sadness and disappointment. My thoughts would sound like: 'Why are you being so mean to me? I do everything for you. I'm not talking to you anymore.' I would catch myself giving a disappointed glance and withdrawing into my shell of feeling sad. I tell you this as someone who has had years and years of training, along with years of personal and professional development in psychology. So if I find it hard, despite all of this knowledge and inner healing work, please know it is so understandable if you do too.

In an ideal world, we would not be triggered by anything, and we would be calm and regulated in our responses. That's just not real life, though – we are all imperfect people just trying to do our best. It also wouldn't be helpful if we were 'perfect' all of the time because our children would probably be frightened of encountering others in their life who understandably 'lose it' now and again. Instead, we should work on trying to catch ourselves when we respond to our children from our emotional brain. Watching how we repair with them after can teach them how to repair with others when they act from their emotional brain.

The best way to help our children with anger and outbursts is first to become extremely self-aware. We might need to reflect on our own childhoods. What were the messages I received growing up about anger? How did my caregivers respond when I felt angry? Did I experience a lot of anger in my home? Were my parents fighting a lot and did I feel afraid? How do I experience anger now? Do I allow myself to experience it or do I push it down? What might be evoked in me when my child expresses their anger?

When we do some inner healing work around this it becomes much easier to externalise the angry behaviour from our child. We don't see an 'angry child' anymore but rather an upset, scared, overwhelmed or distressed child that is using their voice and body to let it all out.

When I am on the receiving end of anger, I tend to feel hopeless and deflated. I might know I have been doing my best and then feel flat and 'what's the point'. I feel like withdrawing from the person (or my child) and going inward into my own world of feeling sad. With a huge amount of self-awareness and self-reflection, while this might sometimes be my immediate response, I am able to catch it quite quickly and reframe the situation in my head. This sounds like: 'Hey! I'm here, Aoife. It's okay – you feel understandably sad here and I know you're only doing your best. Up you get and shake it all out for a minute. You'll be okay soon. Your child is just upset/tired/overwhelmed/pushing boundaries – this is not about you.' This enables me to tune into what they need while also being compassionate to myself.

The greatest guide for managing anger and frustration in our children is to help them find their tears. As Dr Gordon Neufeld teaches, children become stuck in their emotions (especially anger) when they really need to cry but can't access their tears. Emotions need to move to be able to become unstuck. We can help our children hugely here by being a soothing and gentle presence in the face of big feelings. This helps create enough safety for them to allow the tears to fall. If you can, encourage and welcome tears in your family as much as you can. They are so healing and help the painful emotions move and feel seen.

The more we practise tuning in to the need beneath the behaviour, the more it can drastically change how we feel in response to anger. We can remain boundaried with the behaviour, while still being able to connect with the person underneath. This becomes easier and easier the more we do it, but often we might need a little support. Please do reach out to a mental health professional if you are finding this hard. Know that this is not your fault, and our wonderfully complex brains often need some healing and guidance with this.

The repair

For the parents out there who feel like they're walking on eggshells and have acted from their emotional brain (like we all do at times) let's have a look at what the repair might look like.

APOLOGISING

Apologising to our children is never a bad thing, despite what we might have been led to believe in the past. Old-school parenting approaches often said to never apologise, as we have to show our children who is the boss. We now know that apologising to them after periods of reactivity or disconnection is important for our attachment relationship with them. This can be as simple as 'I'm so sorry I got cross with you there. I find it really hard when you scream in my ear like that. It really hurt my ears and I felt sad. I didn't mean to shout back at you – I know you are upset at the moment. I love you.'

CONSIDERING YOUR CHILD'S PERSPECTIVE

We might need to remind ourselves that the anger we are seeing at home could be a build-up of friendship difficulties in school and other peer or sibling dynamics they might be struggling with, as well as their hormones, their awareness of their body image and any unhelpful self-talk they might be experiencing.

We often need to keep letting them know that we are here for them if they would like to talk about anything, reminding them we remember how hard their age can be. If they are really struggling and these periods of reactivity continue happening at home, it might be helpful to link in with a professional to guide you. Your child might find it hard to talk about puberty, their body or other challenges they are experiencing with you, and in those cases an outside person could be a great help. This can always be framed as that you know there might be things they find it difficult to talk to you about and you just want to make sure they have some support.

TIME IN

The most supportive way of connecting with them will always be a 'time in' rather than a 'time out', knowing that all behaviour is communication and trying to look beyond this at their underlying needs. While the outward behaviour might look like it is telling us to 'go away' or to 'leave me alone', underneath they might be feeling, 'I am confused, I feel scared, I don't feel safe'. That is why time outs are rarely an effective way of helping them regulate their emotions. I understand at times this feels impossible and a little 'time out' for the parent is needed while they try to do some deep breathing and help their own nervous system feel more at ease.

Traditional time outs work by removing our child from our presence and putting them in another room or on a 'naughty step' so they can think about their behaviour and why it wasn't helpful. Unfortunately, when we do this we often miss what the behaviour is trying to communicate, and all the child learns is that when they feel scared or things feel 'too much', their caregiver is not there to meet their needs. They are left alone with their feelings, and they often feel unsupported and lonely. They begin to interpret their behaviour as 'bad' and might begin to feel ashamed or abandoned in their pain.

Time in is a much more effective way of helping them learn the future tools of self-regulation. They learn that they can depend on us to meet their needs and that we care enough to figure out the why behind the behaviour. We help them understand that their big feelings are okay and that we can help them figure it out together.

BE KIND TO YOURSELF

And finally, as always, be kind to yourself. They are the best in the world, but our strong-willed little ones can test the most regulated among us! Keep remembering how their determination, persistence, intensity, sensitivity and perceptiveness are what make these little firecrackers spark.

CHAPTER 10

Sensory sensitivities

Understanding our child's sensory profile, and indeed our own, can be a helpful piece of the puzzle in understanding emotions and behaviour. Occupational therapists are the leaders in this field of sensory integration, and I can't speak more highly of their profession. I recommend linking in with them for support if you have a child who is sensory sensitive, and you would like to learn more about this.

Understanding our unique sensory preferences

We all have unique sensory processing and needs. Every human has individual sensory preferences, and it only becomes a sensory challenge when it starts to impact our functioning. Our more sensitive children often have heightened sensitivity to sensory stimuli. This means they may find noises too loud, lights too bright, clothes too itchy or certain food textures challenging.

They might be sensitive to certain smells, and they might need different kinds of movement to regulate their nervous system.

If we are sensitive to sensory stimuli, it makes sense that our nervous system will become overwhelmed by this sensory input from time to time. When our body feels overwhelmed as a result of sensory input from our environment, it activates our threat system and our fight/flight/freeze/fawn response. We often need to reframe our understanding of misbehaviour in our child to an understandable response to sensory overwhelm. We need to understand that meltdowns and challenging behaviour are often stemming from a dysregulated nervous system and that it is not the child's fault. This reframe is one of the most effective and empowering parenting tools we have.

REFLECTING ON OUR OWN SENSORY PROFILE
Before we move on to our children, it might be helpful to think about our own sensory profile. You might relate to the feeling of being 'hangry', how challenging it can be to remain calm and regulated when you feel hungry. Consider how you feel when on public transport and there are lots of smells, and you are squashed in closely with other people. Do you mind if your socks are falling down in your shoe? Do you find woolly jumpers itchy against your skin? How do you feel when you have been in a confined space for too long? How do you feel in loud places? Do you feel calm and relaxed in crowds? Are there any sounds you find it difficult to listen to?

I have what is called misophonia. For anyone who is unsure what this is, misophonia sufferers experience an adverse emotional and physical response to common sounds. These sounds most often relate to the mouth or nasal area but can also be repetitive sounds like a keyboard tapping, pen clicking, cutlery clattering or scraping and so on. The most common trigger sounds appear to be chewing, coughing, sniffing, slurping, drinking, snoring and lip smacking.

The misophonia sufferer experiences a range of emotions in response to these 'trigger sounds', including irritation, anxiety, anger, disgust and rage. It is still unclear in the neuroscientific literature exactly what causes misophonia, but new research shows it appears to be linked to increased activation of the insula and heightened activity of mirror neurons in the brain. We know that sensitive people often have heightened activation in both of these areas so this could be a contributing factor.

Whatever the underlying causes are, it is challenging to live with as the person who has misophonia and for the families of those who have it. I am sad to say I made mealtimes in my family home growing up quite a tense experience for everyone, as I would become visibly agitated with my family as they chewed their food. I tried my best (most of the time) to hide my feelings of anxiety, anger and sometimes rage towards them. I couldn't make sense of this and often wondered why it was happening to me. We could be having a lovely day when suddenly I would hear slurping tea or crunching cereal and my threat response was activated immediately. This manifested as agitation, and I would often feel like I could faint from the stress I experienced inside. This stress would eventually turn into rageful thoughts, and I would imagine causing harm to the person slurping or chewing! This was incredibly confusing for me and so lonely. What kind of person was I that I was imaging hurting someone I love for simply chewing their food? I spent years doing everything I possibly could to manage this – breathing techniques, body-relaxation techniques, challenging my thoughts, practising gratitude and compassion towards others and myself and the list goes on.

This fascinated me as a psychologist, as I came to realise that, yes, emotion-regulation techniques and body work help to an extent but, at the same time, I have a brain that is wired to find certain sounds distressing. This heightened reactivity to these trigger sounds unfortunately would not be solved by emotion-regulation techniques alone. I needed to adapt the environment to my unique sensory profile. I know it probably sounds quite obvious and maybe not that big of a deal, but learning how to adapt the environment to meet my sensory needs has been so liberating. This is exactly what we need to do for our sensory-sensitive children too. If, like me, there are certain sensory stimuli they find stressful and overwhelming, please know that it is okay to help them with this.

I have worked with so many lovely parents who just want the best for their children and say, 'They need to learn how to be in these environments – they have to work on this and continue exposing themselves to it'. But while learning how to regulate ourselves in difficult situations will always be a help, we also need to listen to our sensory profile. Some of us have a brain and nervous system that is wired this way and that is sensory sensitive. This sensitive wiring to the environment means that our body needs to feel safe, first and foremost, before we can engage in any self-regulatory practice. Even for us as adults, it is often impossible to self-regulate when our body is already in a state of high alert. If this is hard for us, we can imagine just how much more difficult this is for our children whose brains are still developing.

We need help to bring our nervous system back into balance by adapting our environment to meet our needs. For me, this is through the use of noise-cancelling ear plugs. I will never forget that day I sat at the dinner table with my family of origin and used ear plugs for the first time. They were so small no one noticed them, and they dulled the noise just enough that I could still hear the conversation, but the chewing sounds were drowned out. I won't pretend I didn't still feel mildly agitated watching the chewing, but I felt one hundred times more at ease. I sat there watching my parents eat their dinner with a sense of relief mixed with shame and sadness. How different my childhood mealtimes would have been if we had access to more information back then about our unique sensory needs. How many tense environments would have been avoided and how much happier our breakfasts and dinners would have been. I finally realised this was not my fault but just the way my nervous system is wired.

REFLECTING ON OUR CHILD'S SENSORY NEEDS

When we really understand our child's unique sensory needs, we can create environments where they can thrive. With this new wisdom, we might reflect on our child and on how we can help them feel less reactive towards sensory stimuli they find challenging. Let's have a look at Rosie's story.

> Rosie is a three-year-old who is sensitive to bright lights, crowds and loud noises. She is a very sociable and active child and loves being out and about and on the go! This is a challenge sometimes because often being out and about means she is exposed to the sensory stimuli she finds difficult. While she might initially feel joy and excitement about an outing, this can quickly turn to meltdowns and wanting to go back home. Her family are unsure what to do and have been hoping continuous exposure to these situations will eventually help these challenges ease. They are feeling exasperated and deflated, as they have had to leave so many social settings as a result of Rosie's distress and are continuously receiving comments from family members that this is just manipulation and misbehaviour. Their families are telling them that they need to stop pandering to Rosie every time she wants to go home and that she needs to learn how to live in the world she is in!
>
> Rosie's family decide to try something new. They buy a pair of noise-cancelling headphones and a pair of sunglasses she likes the feel of on her face. They explain to Rosie how understandable it is that she finds these situations difficult, and it's because that cool big brain of hers is taking in so much from her surroundings. This is her superpower, but it can also be hard – taking in so much information from the environment can make

everything feel a bit overwhelming. They tell her from now on she can wear her magic headphones and sunglasses and see if this helps her. They are apprehensive themselves but are willing to try anything.

The next social gathering they attend is her cousin's party in the garden. It is a sunny day, and they know lots of people will be there. Her parents feel anxious internally but show a united front to Rosie: they tell her they believe in her and if things feel too much she can let them know.

What happens next surprises them. Rosie walks confidently into the party with her magic headphones and sunglasses on. She runs out to the garden and appears to be happily playing outside with her cousins. Her parents can hear her telling them all about her magic headphones and how they help her. Not too long after this, Rosie appears with her headphones and hands them back to her parents. They ask her if she is sure she doesn't need them and she says, 'I'm okay now, thanks.' She runs back outside to her cousins and plays happily for another thirty minutes. Her parents can see she looks tired, and when the music is turned up a little louder, they notice Rosie appears to become more agitated. They ask her if she would like her headphones and she pops them back on.

Rosie is learning how to make adaptations to her environment to meet her needs with sensory stimuli that can feel overwhelming. When her body feels safe enough in this environment, she decides she can manage without the adaptations. When tiredness hits, along with heightened sensory input, she accepts the help of adaptations to her environment again. She is learning how to tune in to her needs to help her feel regulated and at ease.

A more detailed glance at our senses

Most of us have learned that we have five senses. These are our sense of touch, sight, hearing, taste and smell. We actually have eight senses, the other three being our proprioceptive sense, our vestibular sense and our interoceptive sense.

TOUCH

Some of our sensitive children may find certain tactile input challenging. We might notice this from how dysregulated they become in response to textures, if they appear to be upset or have meltdowns. My eldest will be pushed so quickly out of his window of tolerance if his clothes are in any way wet or damp. My youngest will cry immediately if a jumper feels too tight against his skin. We may observe, even very early on, that they find certain clothing uncomfortable on their skin or dislike different textures in food. They might have difficulty with certain temperatures against their skin, so things like baths or changing nappies and clothes can be experienced as stressful. This gets easier when they get older and can communicate with us, but as babies it is much more challenging. There is often a little trial and error with this as we figure out what clothing they find most comfortable and identify patterns in their sensory profile. Some children will have a preference for light gentle touch and for some, light touching can be experienced as threatening for their nervous system. If this is the case for your child, firm-pressure touch will be much more regulating.

Unfortunately, many schools have a requirement to wear a uniform, which can be a real challenge for children with tactile sensitivity. We might identify that their uniform has contributed to discomfort throughout the day, so we can have comfy clothes for them to change into when they get home. One fantastic thing we can do here too is adapt the uniform to meet our child's needs as best we can. Many retailers stock seamless, tagless undershirts. The tighter the compression they have, the more comfortable they will feel and the more regulating for the child's nervous system, as they are receiving that deep-pressure input. It is helpful to discuss this with their school too, explaining you have a child who is an over-responder to certain tactile stimuli. Schools are often a great help at adjusting expectations to meet the needs of the child if we have a shared goal of improving overall functioning, knowing that when children feel comfortable in their sensory and emotional system, it will be easier for them to manage the daily stressors of school.

SIGHT

Some of our children will be sensitive to visual stimuli. They might find lights too bright or be sensitive to the sun in their eyes. We might need to adjust the light settings in our homes if certain light fixtures are visually stressful for them. Soft lighting and dimmed lights can help in these situations. Lava lamps can be a regulating visual tool, as their slow, controlled movements help our nervous system feel more at ease.

For our older children who are in school, it might be helpful to speak to their teachers about positioning them away from the window or allowing them to wear lightly tinted sunglasses if the room is full of natural light. They may become easily distracted and overwhelmed by visual stimuli in their environment, such as movement and different colours. I love being at concerts, but they are a good example of how challenging this can be, as you are so focused on all of the different faces, flashing lights and fast-changing movements in your eyeline. This can be experienced as dysregulating to a nervous system that has a heightened awareness of visual input. We can help our children learn how it feels in their body when they are becoming overwhelmed by visual input and how to use their visual supports.

SMELL

Some of our children will be hypersensitive to certain smells. This can be a challenge, as we are never sure what smells we will encounter in school, out with friends, in restaurants and so on. Sometimes the combination of different smells can be experienced as distressing for a child with smell sensitivity. Something that can really help is having a little soothe kit ready for when they feel overwhelmed by this. A top with your smell or a scent from home can help ground their senses. For younger children, a blanket or their favourite teddy can provide soothing and comfort. As they grow, adding things like essential oils to their soothe kit can be an effective regulation tool. You might sit down with them and brainstorm some ideas to help them with this.

TASTE

Some of our children will have heighted sensitivities to certain tastes. They may find these tastes aversive, and they might set off a little alarm in their fight/flight/freeze/fawn response. They may be over-responsive to some flavours and as a result limit their diet to foods and tastes that feel safe for them. This may be a challenge with brushing teeth too, and finding a flavour of toothpaste they do like, or using a flavourless toothpaste, can be really helpful. If your child is struggling with this and you have concerns around their nutritional intake, link in with your GP, an occupational therapist and a dietitian.

SOUND

Some of our children have heightened sensitivity to sound. They might experience certain sounds as distressing and much louder than someone who is not sensitive to sound. A common one that I experience, and many of the children I have worked with, is lots of competing noises being dysregulating. One of my best friends has a phenomenal ability to focus despite many competing stimuli in her environment. I go into her house, and although the radio is on loudly in the kitchen and the television is blaring in the adjoining sitting room, she will still initiate a conversation with me. Internally, my head feels like it is being pulled in ten directions and I feel completely overstimulated. I now realise I need to be proactive in asking people to turn off external stimuli when we are talking or turn down noises that are distracting. We won't always be able to do this, and in those scenarios, it helps to understand your own nervous system. We should offer ourselves compassion and teach our children how to do this for themselves too. We should help them to not be too hard on themselves in these kinds of situations and suggest using supports like ear defenders.

One question I have been asked a lot is: 'How can I help my child who is sensitive to noise cope with their sibling's crying'? This can be overwhelming for many reasons. Sensitive children have active mirror neurons in their brain that are likely to mirror the distress their sibling is experiencing. This means they often feel the sadness or upset on a physiological level. Also it is an overwhelming experience to listen to crying as an auditory-sensitive person. One of the most helpful things we can do for these children is to drip feed sensory-calming activities throughout their day so that hopefully, when they are in situations like listening to their sibling crying, their sensory cup still has room in it to manage this difficult situation. We might also help them by having their little tool kit at the ready – providing them access to their noise-cancelling headphones and a special corner of the house that they can go to as a relaxation area. If you have space in your home, tepee tents can be brilliant for this. Inside, they can have their cosy blankets, toys, books and anything else that helps them feel at ease. If you don't have the room for this, you can still have a separate area in your living space that they can go to when they feel overwhelmed.

PROPRIOCEPTION

Proprioception is our body-awareness sense. It tells us where our body parts are without having to look for them. Proprioceptive sensory input can be extremely regulating, as it calms our nervous system and helps us process sensory information. A practical example of when we can use this might be when our children come home from playschool or school. As adults, we can relate to evenings often being a challenge; due to all the stimulation throughout our day, we are often exhausted and less patient by then. If we feel this ourselves, we can empathise with this being a hard time for our sensory-sensitive children. If they have been in school all day, taking in so much input, possibly not having enough time for movement and play, and managing social dynamics, we might expect that they need time to help their nervous system feel calm. A big indicator that this is what they need is if they are experiencing an overflow of emotions or appear to be particularly withdrawn.

With the best intentions, we might try to engage them in conversation and ask them all about their day. However, we often need to adjust our expectations of our child. They may need more time to slow down and regulate their nervous system after a busy day, and often words will not be the most effective way to do this. Conversation might feel 'too much', and we may see that they have likely 'hit a wall'.

What works for each child will be unique to them, depending on their sensory profile, but proprioceptive input seems to be particularly helpful for most children at these times. This is deep-pressure muscle work without movement-based input – for example, deep-pressure massage, deep-pressure hugs or even a weighted blanket while they relax on the couch. Engaging in 'heavy work' by lifting heavier objects, pushing–pulling (tug-of-war games, wall press-ups) and crawling games can be effective ways of helping their nervous system feel more at ease. Giving this calming deep-pressure input into their sensory system before they engage in something like mealtimes or homework can be really helpful for them.

VESTIBULAR SENSE

The vestibular sense is all about balance and knowing where our body is in space. It's like our brain's way of knowing which way is up or down, even when our eyes are closed. It can be particularly helpful for any of us with sensory seekers to understand the vestibular system. Sensory seekers often crave more sensory input and enjoy activities that provide strong sensations. These are the children who don't want to leave the playground or are running around wildly at the party. They often love crashing into things and enjoy physical play. They may be the children who want to 'go-go-go' constantly and love spinning around, bouncing and rolling, as these activities stimulate the vestibular system and are experienced as stimulating and pleasurable. If you have a sensory seeker, it can be confusing sometimes, as their sensory needs can fluctuate throughout the day. At certain times, rather than looking for more sensory input, they may try to avoid it. Whether they avoid or seek more input, the goal is still the same. They are looking for something to calm and regulate their nervous system.

This may sound a little confusing (it does to me sometimes, too!) and that is why reaching out to an occupational therapist to understand their sensory profile will be hugely beneficial. They have taught me that, while my son loves spinning, the fluid in our ear continues to spin for up to four hours after we have stopped the spinning activity. This can present challenges around bedtime, and we may need to support him with this. They have taught me to stop the vestibular movement in the ear by doing slow, controlled back-and-forth movements. Swinging can be particularly helpful for this. If we don't have access to a swing, we can build rocking movements into the bedtime routine, such as using a balance board or simply rocking back and forth while listening to some calming music.

INTEROCEPTION

Our interoceptive sense refers to our ability to understand our body's physical signals. It is the process of detecting threat and safety from inside our bodies. It alerts us when we are hungry, thirsty, hot, cold, excited, calm, sad, scared and so on. Some children can be under-responsive and find it difficult to label their emotions and to identify feelings like hunger, thirst and when they need to use the toilet. Occupational therapists will be hugely beneficial in helping them with this if you have a child who is similar. In chapter five we mentioned that sometimes our sensitive children over-respond to these internal sensations and perceive feelings in their body as threatening, so they may be more likely to experience physical manifestations of anxiety, nervousness, sadness and anger.

When we feel intense emotion, we often experience a lot of adrenaline and cortisol in our body, our heart rate speeds up, and our breathing becomes shallower. This can be very intense for a child who has a heightened awareness of their physical sensations. So rather than thinking, 'Oh, I'm a bit nervous, so it makes sense that I am finding it hard to breathe', they might interpret this as 'Oh no, I can't breathe. What is happening to me? I can't cope.' And this often escalates into feelings of panic. It might be helpful to read back on chapter five about fear and a deeply feeling nervous system for ideas on how we can help them with this, reminding ourselves to help them become curious detectives about their body and its signals by practising self-awareness, mindfulness, body scans and grounding techniques. Fidget tools can also be a fantastic help for these children in trying to meet their needs consistently throughout the day, the idea being that meeting their needs throughout the day will minimise their emotion dysregulation and stress. These tools help calm and regulate our sensory over-responsive kids.

Empowering our sensory-sensitive children

Many of the children I work with are so hard on themselves for being 'different', and they push through uncomfortable situations so that they appear 'normal' like their friends. To avoid this, we should use language at home that frames this in a positive and accepting manner so that they learn to speak to themselves this way too. If we believe this is something that is wrong with them, we might inadvertently reinforce this idea for them and create feelings of anxiety and shame. Rather, we can model how common and understandable it is to be impacted by sensory input and it is only because they have this 'really cool brain' that picks up on everything so deeply! While that is a fantastic thing, it does mean the environment can feel a little busy and loud sometimes. And that's okay, we will help them with this. I used to feel embarrassed that I couldn't hear or couldn't focus when many conversations were happening at the one time. Now I will happily say, 'I'm so sorry if I appear distracted – it's just because I have a hard time focusing when there are lots of competing noises. Bear with me!' Or I will be proactive in controlling the controllable, like turning down the radio, the TV and so on.

The main piece of the puzzle is being curious about ourselves and our children around what leads to their sensory overwhelm. Our sensory profile and our children's sensory profile is often dynamic, meaning it changes throughout our day. How we feel in the morning might be very different to how we feel after a busy day. I know my misophonia is always worse at the end of a long day, when my sensory cup is beginning to overflow. Knowing the evening can be a trigger for me helps me modify my environment to help with this. Background music makes me feel more at ease when I come in from work. The radio and talking will be experienced as sensory-cup overflow and I will notice I feel agitated or overwhelmed.

Parenting can be very dysregulating for our sensory cups. The visual overwhelm from clutter everywhere, the noise of siblings fighting and children vocalising their stress and the constant physical touching, if you have little koalas like me who want to be in your arms or are pulling at your clothes from the moment you are in the door, are a very understandable recipe for sensory overwhelm. So please go as easy on yourselves as you can and know that it is completely normal if you feel overloaded sometimes.

When we are not attuned to our profiles it is difficult to know what adaptations to our environment we need to make. It might be helpful to reflect on your own profile and what will help you feel even the smallest bit more regulated in these moments. As a family, you might sit down and build a sensory safety tool kit. This involves creating an individualised plan that incorporates sensory input that will help all of you feel more regulated throughout the day. If you are interested in learning more about any of the above, I will direct you towards some wonderful occupational therapists at the end of this book. They really are the leaders in this field of sensory integration, and I can't emphasise enough how empowering understanding our sensory processing can be. 'All behaviour is communication', and so much of our child's behaviour is driven from their sensory needs. Supporting them with this and making accommodations where possible can be so beneficial for their development.

CHAPTER 11

My wish for every parent

I can't believe we are nearing the end of this book. Thank you from the bottom of my heart for sticking with me this far, and I hope it has been a help for you in understanding sensitivity. I also hope it has been clear throughout this book how much compassion I feel towards you all. We really are all just doing the best we can with the resources we have. Parenting our sensitive souls can be rewarding and challenging at the same time, and we can forget how important it is to look after ourselves too. We all know that on an airplane we need to put on our own oxygen mask before we attend to others, yet in the busyness of parenthood, this is something that easily gets lost. The reality is so many of us are tired, and the demands of life and parenting take precedence over ourselves. This is understandable, especially when we need our energy to advocate for our children or to help them manage their swirl of emotions while remaining (somewhat) calm ourselves.

To trust yourself

We live in the era of social media where we have access to 'experts' on most topics. We hear polarising views on what is most helpful for our children, and this often leads to feelings of anxiety and overwhelm. It is hard to trust ourselves when we have seen that 'X is damaging for our child' or 'X is the only approach that will build their self-esteem'. I read something recently that said if you have ever shouted at your child, you have most likely caused a huge rupture in your relationship and wounded your child forever. These kinds of blanket statements make me feel very frustrated. As with any healthy relationship, there will always be ruptures and repairs. That is part of life. But so many parents are living on the edge and in fear about what exactly is the 'right' approach.

While I am incredibly thankful that we have so much knowledge now on attachment theory and how important it is to make our children feel safe, secure, valued, loved and understood, I also worry that some of this research and knowledge has been misunderstood, taken to extremes and used to shame any parent who may feel exasperated and depleted sometimes and act from their (very human) emotional brain! I would love for us all to remember that relationships are constantly growing, strengthening and evolving. Our relationship with our child when they are two will look different to our relationship with them when they are six, ten, fourteen, seventeen and so on. We are building the foundations now for how safe they will feel with us throughout their life, but that doesn't mean we will do everything 'perfectly'. And when we inevitably cause ruptures by saying things we wish we hadn't, raising our voice, ignoring and so on, remember that we have opportunities here to look inward and to repair. We are also not the same person we were ten years ago, four years ago and so on. We are always growing and learning, and as long as we stay open to that, we are on the right track.

Trusting ourselves is no easy task when we second guess so many of our responses. I hope this book has helped you a little with this and can guide you in times of self-doubt. Try to remember that you are exactly who your child needs. You are more than enough. Despite what you might believe about yourself, you are your child's whole world. When they go through periods of telling you to go away, that you are the worst parent ever, try to remember that this is all part of growing up. This is most likely nothing to do with you, and these are often the times they really need us the most. Empathy and connection will always be our best friends in these moments.

To avoid self-blame and not be afraid to ask for help

I receive so many messages from parents who are afraid to ask for help because they believe they have caused their baby to be more reactive. They say, 'I was stressed during pregnancy and this stress passed on to them. This is all my fault.' While it is true that prolonged stress during pregnancy can impact the developing brain, there is promising research that shows that, even if we have had a stressful pregnancy and our baby appears a little more stressed as a result, we can rewire this. Our brain architecture is always changing, and it is incredibly malleable during our first few years of life. Consistent and predictable co-regulation from a caregiver that is sensitive to the baby's needs will help bring their stress response back into balance. It is also true that you could be the calmest parent during your pregnancy and still have a baby that comes into this world with a more sensitive and reactive nervous system. I remember trying to manage my stress levels as best I could throughout my own pregnancy. Even still, my sensitive little man came into this world responding to it more intensely due to his highly sensitive temperament. He experienced his emotions so deeply that he was pushed out of his window of tolerance very quickly, and this was just the way his wonderful brain was wired.

If you are struggling during the perinatal period, I wish I could jump through this book to comfort you. At one of the most vulnerable times in our lives, the overwhelm and stress that occur with a sensitive baby can be all-encompassing. I know many sensitive children who were relaxed and easy-going babies, but some come into this world experiencing their emotions so intensely that it doesn't take much to activate their little threat system. Being the parent of a sensitive baby who is in distress so often really is excruciating. I work with many parents who have a diagnosis of perinatal depression and anxiety. For some of these parents, when we explore this further, they are experiencing a very understandable reaction to stressful circumstances. Having a baby who is hard to soothe can cause even the most regulated person to move out of their window of tolerance.

It is so easy to doubt yourself, judge yourself or feel completely depleted and like you have nothing left to give. But I promise you it won't always feel this hard. While every developmental stage has its challenges for all children, it really does get easier the more they can understand, so do try to trust your baby and yourself. They are often the babies who don't want to be anywhere but in our arms. I know it is often an incredibly exhausting season, but it will pass. Try to ask for support where you can and please don't suffer alone. Reach out to your GP and find perinatal support services in your area. There are many free services we can access online if we are struggling with our mental health and have financial difficulties. It breaks my heart to think of so many families feeling alone and like they are failing. Please know that your sensitive baby is just more heightened to the world, and this is not your fault. Society and sadly sometimes even health professionals tend to view perinatal mental health problems as an intrinsic problem with the parent. They perceive that the parent has a biological difficulty that is causing this or that it's a reflection of their ability to cope, how they talk to themselves and so on. We don't always formulate our understanding to include the parent's own temperament or neurodivergence, the baby's temperament and how understandably stressful this experience might be, along with how supported the parent is in their environment.

To establish connections and the confidence to hold boundaries

When we really believe what we are doing is right for our children, it is easier to set boundaries with other well-intentioned people in our life. I hope this book has provided you with more confidence in trusting your gut and knowing our more sensitive children often need a different approach. Feeling unsupported or misunderstood can evoke painful feelings in us. When this happens, we may have a tendency to withdraw and go into our own shell. Or we may notice we feel reactive and defensive. Both patterns of coping are ways of protecting us from further feelings of sadness, loneliness, shame and fear. Our need as humans to feel accepted, loved and understood is vital for our emotional well-being. When these needs go unmet it is understandable that we might not feel like ourselves. We likely engage in coping protectors to avoid the painful feelings underneath. Having other people in our life who understand helps us feel connected to ourselves and to others. This can be a real challenge if the people in our life are questioning our parenting and make comments that leave us feeling less than or sad or touch on painful feelings of shame.

We might need to practise tuning into our own needs in relationships and actively work on those needs being met. This is often the tricky part of allowing ourselves to be vulnerable with friends and family. If you are finding things challenging and notice you try to keep going despite feeling overwhelmed, it might be helpful to be open with somebody you trust. You might need to have difficult conversations with loved ones and let them know their actions or behaviours are contributing to painful feelings. And ask them to trust your judgement and that you know your child best. Trusting ourselves becomes easier when we understand the research on brain development and sensitivity. Here are some common scenarios you might find yourself in where it would be helpful to set a boundary:

- *'You are going to spoil her if you pick her up every time she is "upset". She knows exactly what she is doing, and you are just reinforcing her behaviour!'*
  'I can see why you might think that. It can certainly feel that way sometimes, I know. But small children don't have the cognitive capacity to be manipulative – they just act from their emotional brain. Rather than spoiling her, I am actually helping her regulate her emotions and to understand she can depend on me during times of stress. I have been practising trying to look past the behaviour to the feeling underneath.'
- *'I don't understand why you won't be stricter with him; you need to show him who is in charge.'*
  'I get it! It's frustrating that he keeps doing the thing we don't want him to do. Unfortunately, though, he doesn't understand yet why that might be dangerous or breakable. By raising our voice, we might scare him into not doing it again, but he hasn't actually learned a lesson. Young children lack impulse control, so it's easier for us to continue saying a gentle and firm no and redirecting them at this stage.'
- *'You should really punish her when she hits like that! It's not okay.'*
  'I hear you – it can be really triggering for me when she does this too. Children often act out their frustrations with their body. They haven't learned how to regulate their emotions yet, and when they "act out" that is often quite literally what they are doing: acting out their feelings. It's more helpful to

try and connect with what the frustration, sensory need or upset might be instead of being shaming or punishing about their behaviour.'

- *'He is getting way too old for this – it's not normal that his separation anxiety is so high.'*

  'All children go at their own pace! Some of our sensitive souls continue to need us during times that feel scary for them. This is okay for me, and please don't say things like that around him. There is nothing wrong with him; his sensitive nervous system takes longer to adjust to new things.'

- *'You should really force her to eat more vegetables! Her diet is not good enough. Let her go hungry and then she will eat a better range of foods.'*

  'She's doing her best. She's sensitive to textures in food, and new tastes take a while to get used to. I keep offering different foods, but the ones she eats most are safe and consistent for her. I am confident in our food choices, so I will ask you to respect that, please.'

I could go on, but I hope these give you some ideas for holding boundaries with people in your life.

I am a firm believer that knowledge is power. If you can, link in with a psychologist, an occupational therapist, a feeding specialist, a GP and anyone who can help provide you with the correct information on the choices you are making for your child. We might have to ask them if they have experience with sensitive children and make sure they are a neuroaffirmative professional. Many healthcare professionals are fantastic but may not have experience or training in working with sensitive children, so the advice we get might not be relevant or might not be a holistic approach for our child.

To be mindful of comparison traps and remember that it's okay to take your time

Comparison traps often fuel our anxiety as parents. You might see other children diving in immediately in new places or with new activities, while your child might need that little bit more time. One thing that can be so helpful for us and our children is to believe in them but also adjust our expectations on their pace, as illustrated in this story about our swimming pool.

It fascinated me watching just how differently my two children approached the swimming pool. My younger son saw it and laughed in delight, pulling his hand from mine and racing towards the edge of the pool, ready to jump in head first. Thankfully, I managed to catch him before he did this! Forgetting to put armbands on a mischievous sensory-seeking toddler was not the best idea I have ever had. My elder son approached the pool with caution, tentatively watching the others as they jumped in and splashed around. For a few weeks, we sat at the edge of the baby pool while he stuck his feet in the water, not quite ready for his body to be submerged. As the weeks progressed, he became more confident and felt brave enough to go into the big pool once he was being supported in my arms. He still doesn't feel comfortable enough to swim with an inflatable support and not holding on to me, but I have no doubt we will get there in time.

His brother, on the other hand, is frustrated at being held and dunks his head into the water every chance he gets, coming up for air while spluttering mouthfuls of water and simultaneously finding it all hilarious. My elder son wears his goggles on his head, and my sense is we are a while away from his being comfortable in going anywhere near under the surface. It's intriguing to see these different temperaments at play, and I feel grateful I am not putting pressure on this to be any different. It is important to remind ourselves to put ourselves in their shoes. I watch in admiration at how brave my son is to continue to come to the pool despite finding it all a little scary and overwhelming.

When we continue encouraging them and supporting them through these new skills, they learn how to celebrate their efforts. We need to trust that they will get there when they are ready, and these little pushes from us, by continuing to go despite it being hard, help their confidence grow. It is so helpful here to tell them how proud we are of them: 'Well done going into the pool again today, love! I am so proud of you – I know it's not easy. You made such a brilliant effort, and we spent even longer in there today than last week. Go you!' Sometimes we forget how important these little reminders are for them. It is understandable that internally you might be comparing your child to others, and maybe you have said things in times of frustration like: 'Come on! All the other boys and girls are doing it – why can't you?' Please go easy on yourself if you were sucked into the comparison trap and reacted from this vulnerable place. We are all only human! A little mantra I love that my own mom used to always say to me is to remember that 'tomorrow is a new day'.

To find ways to bring more play and fun into your life

Our more sensitive souls can be a little serious sometimes. All of that reflecting, noticing and deep-thinking can translate into seriousness and being lost in their own thoughts. The same goes for us as parents. It can be hard to remember how important laughter is and how incredible play is for our soul.

I am not the most naturally playful person. I can be at times, but like our sensitive children, I often get lost in my own inner world and interact in the world more 'seriously'. I need to actively remind myself to bring joy and laughter into my day-to-day. Our children have the capacity to feel joy in such deep and meaningful ways, especially our sensitive children who have the ability to feel every emotion so deeply. We can be their biggest teachers with this, and when we notice they are in a serious mood or appear to be lost in the thousand thoughts they may be having, we might help shift their energy to play.

List three things you love to do, the things that make you smile. Reflect on your week and ask yourself: 'Am I building in enough things that fill up my own cup? Do I have enough opportunity to laugh and play in my own day-to-day? What is one small thing I could incorporate into my week this week that will make me smile?'

It might be helpful to reflect on your own experience of childhood and what your memories of play are. Do you remember being played with when you were small? What did this look like, and how did it feel? So many adults I work with can't remember or feel far removed from their playful self. If this is you too, just know that we all have it in there somewhere. As Dr Gordon Neufeld wisely says:

> Children at play are insulated from the alarming world around them. Play is a sanctuary of safety. Play is the original school, far more effective than anything society could possibly invent. Rather than try to make the home a school, it would be much more important in these times to make the home a true playground where nature can take care of all of us.

For our younger children, this might be by pretending to eat their toes, by playing the tickle-monster game with their consent. A firm favourite in our house is smelling their feet and having a huge reaction to this by falling on the floor from their feet being 'so smelly'. Watching them roll round in delight at this game really helps ground me in the present too. Oxytocin and dopamine flow through our systems when we engage our 'silliness'. Chasing games can be fun, hide and seek too, and another firm favourite for us is rough and tumble, where we pretend to be airplanes or jump off the couch onto cushions pretending we are 'diving down into the sea'.

As they grow, singing, making up dances together, acting out their favourite stories, going to the beach, scavenger hunts in your home or garden, throwing or kicking a ball back and forth are all simple ideas that keep us connected. The goal is that they are involved in something 'just for fun', where rules and competing are not the main focus. My biggest piece of advice to any parent of a sensitive child is to find out what makes them smile. And when you do, let that be one of the most important things that guide you on this journey. Do it more and more and more and more. Finally, remember as best you can how important you are too. Maybe you have had a very busy day, then you come home, cook dinner, do bath time, do bedtime and finally sit down yourself. It is understandable that you might just switch on the TV and zone out for a few hours before bed. But if you haven't paused to intentionally regulate your stress response, that adrenaline and cortisol will still be pumping through your system. Releasing stress doesn't have to be a huge or arduous process, or another 'task' you have to complete. It might be simply taking a few deep breaths, going for a walk, having a bath, engaging in deep-pressure hugs or putting on a weighted blanket and simultaneously saying something like 'mind slowing down' on your in-breath and 'body slowing down' as you exhale. It can be helpful to repeat this a few times as you allow yourself to slow down at last.

Finally, from the bottom of my heart, thank you a million times for reading my book. I am sending you all so much love, strength and kindness from one caregiver doing their best to another. Take good care of yourselves and remember that these children are precious and if we listen closely, we can learn so much from them. There is such beauty in emotional depth and these children are often so creative, passionate, loyal and intuitive. I know it's hard sometimes; I am right there with you and please never forget how important you are too. I also understand there may be hard times navigating life as these kids need a different approach than is the 'norm' in our culture. So, trust yourself and trust your child. Let's be their advocates, their guides and most importantly their biggest support. I will be thinking of you all.

Further resources

For more reading on sensitivity, I highly recommend Dr Elaine Aron's books. I have learnt so much from her and she is one of the most prominent thought leaders in this field. You can find more about her fantastic work and a list of her brilliant books on her website: www.hsperson.com.

For current research and up-to-date learnings by some of the key researchers in this area such as Professor Michael Pluess, Dr Francesa Lionetti and others, I highly recommend www.sensitivityresearch.com.

Chapter 10 of this book has been guided by key learnings from the wonderful work of my friends at Everyday OT (www.everydayotireland.com). They are so inspirational and are helping so many of us understand just how important our child's sensory system is. They really are a wealth of knowledge in this field, and I can't recommend the resources available on their website any more highly. They have a webinar called 'Becoming a Sensory Detective' that is particularly helpful in understanding how to help your sensory sensitive child.

For practical support and resources on helping your sensitive child to manage anxiety and other big emotions, Rebecca Quin's resource hub is an excellent tool. She has downloadable guides and exercises for families available through her website www.thepsychologypractice.ie. Rebecca is one of the most knowledgeable and kind psychologists you could meet and shares brilliant tips for parents on her Instagram page @rebeccaquin.

Rachel Samson is an incredibly gifted and talented consulting clinical psychologist working with sensitive children and adults. I have been privileged to speak at conferences and run courses with Rachel and she is an expert in the field of sensitivity. For a list of further resources from Rachel please check out her Instagram @australianpsychologist.

If you need any help with navigating the world of sleep, I can't recommend Dr Emma Bagnall, Rachael Shepard and Rachel Samson any more highly. They are all highly skilled clinicians with extensive expertise in supporting neurodivergent and sensitive children with sleep. Dr Emma Bagnall's website is www.themotheringpsychologist.com and she can be found on Instagram @themotheringpsychologist. Rachael Shepard's website is www.heysleepybaby.com and she can be found on Instagram @heysleepybaby. Rachel Samson's details are above.

If you are a professional who is working with families and would like to learn more about how to support them with their child's sleep, I highly recommend Louise Herbert's wonderful course. She is the director of the Certification in Paediatric Sleep and Development and specialises in empowering families of sensitive children. This is a fully accredited qualification and is the only one of its kind that is accredited globally and across sectors. I am honoured to be a guest speaker on this certification on highly sensitive children. The details can be found at www.mothernourishnurture.com.

For an excellent article on sleep training, I recommend reading Amanda Ruggeri's article 'What really happens when babies are left to cry it out?' listed below. She is a BBC journalist who covers a range of topics and provides a balanced and nuanced view of the research on sleep: https://www.bbc.com/future/article/20220322-how-sleep-training-affects-babies. You can follow her work on Instagram @mandyruggeri.

For guides on the risks and how to engage in safe co-sleeping, I recommend following the 'safe sleep seven'. Details can be found on the La Leche League International website: https://llli.org/breastfeeding-info/sleep-bedshare/.

Michelle Charriere, MAS-IFP is an infant mental health specialist who has a huge number of resources available on her website www.babiesandbrains.com or on her Instagram page @babiesandbrains. Michelle is highly skilled and trained in mental health for children and is the person to link in with if you are having any difficulties navigating childcare for your sensitive child. She also empowers parents on understanding the importance of connection and fostering secure attachment relationships.

Dr Kimberley Bennett is a well-respected senior clinical psychologist with a passion for supporting sensitive children and their families. She has many resources on her website including webinars on helping your child to adjust to a new sibling, a blog on guiding your sensitive child with screen time and courses on separation anxiety and managing big emotions. Her details are www.thepsychologistschild.com or on Instagram @thepsychologistschild.

For ideas on how to connect with our children through play, I highly recommend Dr Joanna Fortune or Hayley Rice. Joanna has many books available to guide you through every age and developmental stage and Hayley offers many brilliant webinars, along with running a successful community membership. Joanna's details are on www.solamh.com and on Instagram @drjoannafortune. Hayley's website is www.hayley-rice.com and her Instagram is @hayley_rice_.

If you are hoping to engage in psychological assessment or therapy for your child, I can highly recommend Dr Claire Conlon, and Dr Marese McDonnell and Dr Joanna Clancy. They are extremely neuroaffirmative and have such a gentle approach in the way they support families with both assessment and therapeutic input. Claire's website is www.thecaterpillarclinic.com and her Instagram is @thecaterpillarclinic. Marese and Joanna can be found at www.cradlepsychology.com and on Instagram @cradlepsychology.

For everyday practical ideas on how to mind our own nervous system as parents, I highly recommend the work of my lovely friend Allison Keating. She has just published her wonderful book *It's All Too Much* and aims to help us all to slow down, and tune into what we need and what is truly important in this fast-paced and busy world. For more details I recommend following her Instagram @thepracticalpsychologist.

Bibliography

Aron, E.N. (1996). *The Highly Sensitive Person: How to Thrive When the World Overwhelms You.* New York: Broadway Books.

Aron, E.N. (2012). *The Highly Sensitive Child: Helping our children thrive when the world overwhelms them.* HarperCollins UK.

Badenoch, B., & Porges, S.W. (2023). *The Heart of Trauma: Healing the Embodied Brain in the Context of Relationships.* Wiley.

Belsky, J., & Pluess, M. (2009). 'The Nature (and Nurture?) of Plasticity in Early Human Development.' *Perspectives on Psychological Science*, 4(4), 345–351. https://doi.org/10.1111/j.1745-6924.2009.01136.x

Belsky, J. (2013). 'Differential Susceptibility to Environmental Influences.' *International Journal of Child Care and Education Policy/International Journal of Child Care and Education*, 7(2), 15–31. https://doi.org/10.1007/2288-6729-7-2-15

Blascovich, J., & Spencer, S.J. (2004). 'Contextual cues and the other-race effect in face perception.' *Journal of Personality and Social Psychology*, 86(2), 235-247. https://doi.org/10.1037/0022-3514.86.2.235

Boyce, W.T. (2019). *The Orchid and the Dandelion: Why Sensitive People Struggle and How All Can Thrive.* Pan Macmillan.

Brown, Brené. (2010) 'The power of vulnerability.' [Dataset]. In PsycEXTRA Dataset. https://doi.org/10.1037/e517042011-001

Brown, Brené. (2012). 'Daring Greatly: How the Courage to Be Vulnerable Transforms the Way We Live, Love, Parent, and Lead.' https://ci.nii.ac.jp/ncid/BB12851855

Brown, Brené. (2021). *Atlas of the Heart: Mapping Meaningful Connection and the Language of Human Experience.* Random House.

Chess, S., & Thomas, A. (1996). *Temperament: Theory and practice.* New York: Brunner/Mazel.

Davidson, R.J., & McEwen, B.S. (2012). 'Social influences on neuroplasticity: Stress and interventions to promote well-being.' *Nature Neuroscience*, 15(5), 689–695. https://doi.org/10.1038/nn.3087

Dozier, T.H., & Noren, G.S. (2020). 'Neural mechanisms underlying misophonia: A review of neuroimaging studies.' *Frontiers in Psychology*, 11, 601. https://doi.org/10.3389/fpsyg.2020.

Ellis, B.J., & Boyce, W.T. (2008). 'Biological Sensitivity to Context.' *Current Directions in Psychological Science*, 17(3), 183–187. https://doi.org/10.1111/j.1467-8721.2008.00571.x

Ellis, B.J., Boyce, W.T., Belsky, J., Bakermans-Kranenburg, M.J., & Van Ijzendoorn, M.H. (2011). 'Differential susceptibility to the environment: An evolutionary–neurodevelopmental theory.' *Development and Psychopathology*, 23(1), 7–28. https://doi.org/10.1017/s0954579410000611

Gerhardt, S. (2004). *Why Love Matters: How Affection Shapes a Baby's Brain*. Routledge.

Hoffman, M.L. (2000). *Empathy and moral development: Implications for caring and justice*. New York: Cambridge University Press.

Johnstone, L. (2018). 'The Power Threat Meaning Framework: An alternative to psychiatric diagnosis.' In R. Clare & M. Simmonds (Eds.), *Critical Perspectives on Mental Health and Psychiatry: An Introduction* (pp. 181–202). Routledge.

Jolicoeur-Martineau, A., Belsky, J., Szekely, E., Widaman, K.F., Pluess, M., Greenwood, C., & Wazana, A. (2019). 'Distinguishing differential susceptibility, diathesis-stress, and vantage sensitivity: Beyond the single gene and environment model.' *Development and Psychopathology*, 32(1), 73–83. https://doi.org/10.1017/s0954579418001438

Keysers, C., et al. (2008). 'The mirror neuron system.' *Social Neuroscience*, 3(3–4), 193–198. https://doi.org/10.1080/17470910802408513

Lionetti, F., Pastore, M., Moscardino, U., Nocentini, A., Pluess, K., & Pluess, M. (2019). 'Sensory Processing Sensitivity and its association with personality traits and affect: A meta-analysis.' *Journal of Research in Personality*, 81, 138–152. https://doi.org/10.1016/j.jrp.2019.05.013

McKenna, J.J., & Ball, H.L. (2010). *Sleeping with your baby: A parent's guide to co-sleeping.* New York: Berkley Books.

Middlemiss, W., Granger, D.A., Goldberg, W.A., & Nathans, L. (2012). 'Asynchrony of mother–infant hypothalamic–pituitary–adrenal axis activity following extinction of infant crying responses induced during the transition to sleep.' *Early Human Development*, 88(4), 227–232.

NICHD Early Child Care Research Network. (2006). *Child care and child development: Results of the NICHD study of early child care and youth development.* New York: Guilford Press.

Perry, B.D., & Dobson, C.L. (2008). 'The neurosequential model of therapeutics.' *Reclaiming Children and Youth*, 17(3), 38–43. http://childtrauma.org/wp-content/uploads/2013/08/NMT_Article_08.pdf

Perry, B.D. (2009). 'Examining Child Maltreatment Through a Neurodevelopmental Lens: Clinical Applications of the Neurosequential Model of Therapeutics.' *Journal of Loss and Trauma*, 14(4), 240–255. https://doi.org/10.1080/15325020903004350

Pluess, M., & Belsky, J. (2010). 'Differential susceptibility to parenting and quality child care.' *Developmental Psychology*, 46(2), 379–390. https://doi.org/10.1037/a0015203

Pluess, M., & Boniwell, I. (2015). 'Sensory-Processing Sensitivity predicts treatment response to a school-based depression prevention program: Evidence of Vantage Sensitivity.' *Personality and Individual Differences*, 82, 40–45. https://doi.org/10.1016/j.paid.2015.03.011

Pluess, M., & Belsky, J. (2015). 'Vantage sensitivity: genetic susceptibility to effects of positive experiences'. *Genetics of Psychological Well-being*, 193–210. Oxford University Press. https://doi.org/10.1093/acprof:oso/9780199686674.003.0012

Porges, S.W. (2001). 'The polyvagal theory: Phylogenetic contributions to social behavior'. *Physiology & Behavior*, 79(3), 503–513. Elsevier. https://doi.org/10.1016/S0031-9384(03)00156-2

Porges, S.W. (2011). *The Polyvagal Theory: Neurophysiological Foundations of Emotions, Attachment, Communication, and Self-regulation*. W.W. Norton.

Porges, S.W., & Dana, D. (2018). *Clinical Applications of the Polyvagal Theory: The Emergence of Polyvagal-Informed Therapies*. W.W. Norton.

Siegel, D.J., & Hartzell, M. (2011). *Parenting from the inside out: How a deeper self-understanding can help you raise children who thrive*. New York: TarcherPerigee.

Smith, J. (2023). *Inspirational quotes for growth*. Motivational Press.

Strack, F., Martin, L.L., & Stepper, S. (1988). 'Inhibiting and facilitating conditions of the human smile: A nonobtrusive test of the facial feedback hypothesis'. *Journal of Personality and Social Psychology*, 54(5), 768–777. https://doi.org/10.1037/0022-3514.54.5.768

Acknowledgements

Firstly, I would like to thank Sarah Liddy, publisher at Gill Books, for taking a chance on me. I will never forget the day I received an email in my inbox from you asking to meet to discuss a potential book. I was so honoured to even be invited to a meeting but, truthfully, never in my dreams did I believe I would be lucky enough to be here now writing my acknowledgments. Sarah, thank you from the bottom of my heart for believing in me and in the words I have to share. Thank you for being so supportive during this whole process, I will be forever grateful.

My warmest and most heartfelt thanks to managing editor, Margaret Farrelly. From the moment we met I could tell you understood the message I wanted to share. Working with you has been so seamless, and it was so comforting knowing I had someone so wise, knowledgeable and kind reading over my words. You made writing this book such an enjoyable process Margaret, and I will never be able to thank you enough.

Thank you to Emma Dunne, Charlie Lawlor, Kristen Olson

and all of the rest of the team at Gill Books who do such a brilliant job of bringing all of the important pieces together. I appreciate you all.

To my incredible husband Michael, thank you so much for everything. Thank you for being so patient with my intense hyperfocus when I put my mind to something. I know that is not easy! Thank you for taking the boys to countless playgrounds while I tried to squeeze in an extra hour of writing here and there. You are the rock in my life and my best friend. Thank you for being the best dad to the boys and for believing in me, your support means the world to me.

To my wonderful children, Oscar and Ollie, thank you for inspiring me daily. I love you both more than words could ever say. I never knew my heart could grow to the size it has since you were both born. Your little brother will be so lucky to have you both as his guides in life and I can't wait to watch you grow. I feel like the luckiest person in the whole world that you two little angels picked me as your mom.

To my mom and dad, thank you so much for believing in me and for being the biggest support and encouragement a daughter could have. I have never met anyone else who gets as excited about 'the little things' as you do. I know this book is most definitely one of the 'big' things, but I can never tell you how much I appreciate how you have made me feel about these achievements along the way. I will never be able to thank you enough for everything you have done for me and for believing in me.

To my sister Aisling, how can I ever thank you enough for just being you? You are part of my heart and soul, and I am forever grateful for your friendship. I am so proud of you, thank you for always being the biggest believer in me and for inspiring me every day. I wouldn't be me without you. Dave, thank you for everything too and for being such an amazing person, I can't wait to have you both home and for all of our adventures to come.

To Helen, Sarah and JOMI, thank you for your endless help with school drop-offs, cooked dinners and organising, and all of your ongoing support this year and always. We appreciate you so much and we would be completely lost without you! We love you all.

To my amazing gran, I love you with all of my heart. Thank you for being such an inspiration to us all and for showing us what true resilience looks like.

To my colleagues, friends and team in St Patrick's Mental Health Services, particularly my supervisor and close friend Dr Rachel Egan and my director Dr Clodagh Dowling. Thank you for your unwavering support and encouragement while writing this book and for all of your compassion and kindness. Dr Violet Johnstone, thank you for everything and for sharing your knowledge with me over the years. Thank you so much Dr Jessica O'Sullivan for all of the laughs and for your friendship. And finally, thank you to Dr Sarah O'Dwyer for your belief in me throughout the year and for making me feel so welcome on your team. You are all very special people.

Thank you so much to Dr Susan Simpson for all of your support and encouragement and for being the first person to point me in the direction of the research on high sensitivity. I have admired you for years and always hoped one day I would find something to be as passionate about as you are with your work. I have you to thank for helping me discover my 'why' and I am so grateful.

Thank you, a million times, to Dan Roberts, my wonderful supervisor and fellow sensitive soul. Thank you for being such a huge support to me this year. Your empathic, nurturing and wise presence has been a guiding light to me during times of self-doubt and worry. I know you are in 'my corner' and your encouragement and belief in me has meant the world. You are such an inspiration.

Sarah Crosby, I am not even sure where to start in how to thank you for all of your kindness and guidance this year. I feel so lucky to have met you and will be forever grateful for your support.

My lecturers and supervisors in Trinity College Dublin, thank you for such an incredible learning journey and for sharing your expertise with me.

To my best friends. Some of you I have been lucky to meet in more recent years, and some of us have been together since we were small, I would be so lost without you all. I am eternally grateful for your friendship and my life would look very different without you in it. Thank you for all of the laughs, for all of the cries and for being the best supporters a friend could have. I feel like I have won life's lottery having you by my side through thick and thin.

Last, but most certainly not least, thank you to my beautiful clients. To all the sensitive little (and big) souls whom I have had the greatest privilege of learning from. Thank you for allowing me into the depths of your inner world and for trusting me with your hearts. The world will always be that little bit kinder and that little bit softer with you in it.

Notes